Visit Christian Art Gifts, Inc. at www.christianartgifts.com.

Wisdom from the Word for Women

Published by Christian Art Gifts, Inc., under license from Tyndale House Publishers, Inc.

Previously published as *TouchPoints for Women: God's Answers for Your Daily Needs*.
First printing by Tyndale House Publishers, Inc., in 1996.

Second edition questions and notes copyright © 2011 by Ronald A. Beers. All rights reserved.

First edition copyright © 1996, 1998 by Tyndale House Publishers, Inc.
All rights reserved.

First edition notes and special features copyright © by Ronald A. Beers and V. Gilbert Beers.
All rights reserved.

General editors: Ronald A. Beers, V. Gilbert Beers, Amy Mason

Contributing writers: V. Gilbert Beers, Rebecca Beers, Brian R. Coffey, Jonathan Farrar, Jonathan Gray, Sean A. Harrison, Sandy Hull, Amy E. Mason, Rhonda K. O'Brien, Douglas J. Rumford, Linda Taylor

Cover and interior images used under license from Shutterstock.com

Designed by Christian Art Gifts

Scripture quotations are taken from the *Holy Bible*, New Living Translation, copyright © 1996, 2004, 2007 by Tyndale House Foundation. Used by permission of Tyndale House Publishers, Inc., Carol Stream, Illinois 60188. All rights reserved.

Printed in China

ISBN 978-1-4321-3252-1 (LuxLeather)
ISBN 978-1-4321-3279-8 (Hardcover)

20 21 22 23 24 25 26 27 28 29 - 10 9 8 7 6 5 4 3 2 1

Wisdom
FROM THE
WORD

FOR WOMEN

Christian art gifts

Abilities

> To those who use well what they are given,
> even more will be given, and they will
> have an abundance. MATTHEW 25:29

Does God give me talents and abilities for a reason?

The LORD said to Moses, "Look, I have specifically chosen Bezalel ... I have filled him with the Spirit of God, giving him great wisdom, ability, and expertise in all kinds of crafts. He is a master craftsman, expert in working with gold, silver, and bronze. He is skilled in engraving and mounting gemstones and in carving wood." Exodus 31:1-5

When someone has been given much, much will be required in return; and when someone has been entrusted with much, even more will be required. Luke 12:48

Whatever you do, do it all for the glory of God. 1 Corinthians 10:31

How can my God-given abilities have the most impact?

God has given each of you a gift from his great variety of spiritual gifts. Use them well to serve one another. 1 Peter 4:10

Use them for your personal enjoyment, but use them also to serve others, for that is where they have the greatest impact.

Acceptance

> But to all who accepted him, he gave the right to become children of God. JOHN 1:12

I feel so unworthy – does God really accept me?

God created human beings in his own image. In the image of God he created them; male and female he created them. Genesis 1:27

God showed his great love for us by sending Christ to die for us while we were still sinners. Romans 5:8

Even before he made the world, God loved us and chose us in Christ to be holy and without fault in his eyes. God decided in advance to adopt us into his own family by bringing us to himself through Jesus Christ. This is what he wanted to do, and it gave him great pleasure. Ephesians 1:4-5

What makes me acceptable to God?

There is only one God, and he makes people right with himself only by faith, whether they are Jews or Gentiles. Romans 3:30

We know that a person is made right with God by faith in Jesus Christ, not by obeying the law. And we have believed in Christ Jesus, so that we might be made right with God because of our faith in Christ, not because we have obeyed the law. For no one will ever be made right with God by obeying the law. Galatians 2:16

Adoption

> Even before he made the world, God loved us and chose us in Christ to be holy and without fault in his eyes ... This is what he wanted to do, and it gave him great pleasure. So we praise God for the glorious grace he has poured out on us who belong to his dear Son. EPHESIANS 1:4-6

How has God adopted me? Why would he want to do that?

God sent his Son, born of a woman, subject to the law. God sent him to buy freedom for us who were slaves to the law, so that he could adopt us as his very own children.   Galatians 4:4-5

See how very much our Father loves us, for he calls us his children, and that is what we are!   1 John 3:1

God decided in advance to adopt us into his own family by bringing us to himself through Jesus Christ. This is what he wanted to do, and it gave him great pleasure.   Ephesians 1:5

You are a chosen people. You are royal priests, a holy nation, God's very own possession. As a result, you can show others the goodness of God, for he called you out of the darkness into his wonderful light.
1 Peter 2:9

To all who believed [the Father's one and only Son] and accepted him, he gave the right to become children of God.   John 1:12

Affirmation

"The mountains may move and the hills disappear, but even then my faithful love for you will remain. My covenant of blessing will never be broken," says the Lord, who has mercy on you. ISAIAH 54:10

How does God affirm me?

God created human beings in his own image. In the image of God he created them; male and female he created them. Genesis 1:27

[Jesus said,] "I give them eternal life, and they will never perish. No one can snatch them away from me, for my Father has given them to me, and he is more powerful than anyone else. No one can snatch them from the Father's hand." John 10:28-29

God affirmed you when he created you like himself. He values you so much that he was willing to send his Son to die for you because he wants you to live with him forever.

How can I affirm others?

Let us aim for harmony in the church and try to build each other up. Romans 14:19

Encourage each other and build each other up, just as you are already doing … Show [your leaders] great respect and wholehearted love because of their work. And live peacefully with each other. 1 Thessalonians 5:11, 13

The Lord is compassionate and merciful, slow to get angry and filled with unfailing love. PSALM 103:8

How should I deal with my own anger in relationships?

"Don't sin by letting anger control you." Don't let the sun go down while you are still angry. Ephesians 4:26

Get rid of all bitterness, rage, anger … Instead, be kind to each other, tenderhearted, forgiving one another, just as God through Christ has forgiven you. Ephesians 4:31-32

Anger must be dealt with quickly, before it becomes bitter, hateful, or vengeful. As hard as forgiveness might sound, it is most effective in melting anger away.

What is the best way to deal with an angry person?

A gentle answer deflects anger, but harsh words make tempers flare. Proverbs 15:1

Mockers can get a whole town agitated, but the wise will calm anger. Proverbs 29:8

Appearance

> Charm is deceptive, and beauty does not last; but a woman who fears the LORD will be greatly praised. PROVERBS 31:30

How much does appearance matter?

The LORD doesn't see things the way you see them. People judge by outward appearance, but the LORD looks at the heart.
1 Samuel 16:7

Don't be concerned about the outward beauty of fancy hairstyles, expensive jewelry, or beautiful clothes. You should clothe yourselves instead with the beauty that comes from within, the unfading beauty of a gentle and quiet spirit, which is so precious to God.
1 Peter 3:3-4

Women who claim to be devoted to God should make themselves attractive by the good things they do. 1 Timothy 2:10

Is there any value to maintaining a good appearance?

Don't you realize that your body is the temple of the Holy Spirit, who lives in you and was given to you by God? You do not belong to yourself, for God bought you with a high price. So you must honor God with your body. 1 Corinthians 6:19-20

Bible

Your eternal word, O Lord,
stands firm in heaven. PSALM 119:89

How can a book written so long ago be relevant for me today?

All Scripture is inspired by God and is useful to teach us what is true and to make us realize what is wrong in our lives. It corrects us when we are wrong and teaches us to do what is right. God uses it to prepare and equip his people to do every good work. 2 Timothy 3:16-17

How can the Bible give me guidance?

You guide me with your counsel, leading me to a glorious destiny. Psalm 73:24

Your word is a lamp to guide my feet and a light for my path. Psalm 119:105

The Scriptures give us hope and encouragement as we wait patiently for God's promises to be fulfilled. Romans 15:4

The grass withers and the flowers fade, but the word of our God stands forever. Isaiah 40:8

Blessings

Let's not get tired of doing what is good.
At just the right time we will reap a harvest
of blessing if we don't give up. GALATIANS 6:9

How can I receive God's blessings?

How joyful are those who fear the LORD – all who follow his ways! Psalm 128:1

Joyful are those who have the God of Israel as their helper, whose hope is in the LORD their God. Psalm 146:5

Blessed are those who trust in the LORD and have made the LORD their hope and confidence. Jeremiah 17:7

What kinds of blessings does God send my way?

The LORD God is our sun and our shield. He gives us grace and glory. The LORD will withhold no good thing from those who do what is right. Psalm 84:11

Thank God! He gives us victory over sin and death through our Lord Jesus Christ. 1 Corinthians 15:57

Peace, comfort, joy, fellowship with God, hope, and eternal life with him are the best blessings of all – and they have been promised to you.

Boundaries

> Your commands make me wiser than my enemies,
> for they are my constant guide. PSALM 119:98

Why do I need boundaries?

Make me walk along the path of your commands, for that is where my happiness is found. Psalm 119:35

Guide my steps by your word, so I will not be overcome by evil. Psalm 119:133

What are God's boundaries for me?

O people, the LORD has told you what is good, and this is what he requires of you: to do what is right, to love mercy, and to walk humbly with your God. Micah 6:8

What does the LORD your God require of you? He requires only that you fear the LORD your God, and live in a way that pleases him, and love him and serve him with all your heart and soul. And you must always obey the LORD's commands and decrees that I am giving you today for your own good. Deuteronomy 10:12-13

God's boundaries are his loving restraints – his commands – to keep you from falling away from him.

Busyness

Jesus said, "Come to me, all of you who are weary and carry heavy burdens, and I will give you rest. Take my yoke upon you. Let me teach you, because I am humble and gentle at heart, and you will find rest for your souls." MATTHEW 11:28-29

What are the dangers of busyness?

We are merely moving shadows, and all our busy rushing ends in nothing. We heap up wealth, not knowing who will spend it.
Psalm 39:6

Enthusiasm without knowledge is no good; haste makes mistakes.
Proverbs 19:2

How can I find rest from being too busy?

You have six days each week for your ordinary work, but on the seventh day you must stop working, even during the seasons of plowing and harvest. Exodus 34:21

He lets me rest in green meadows; he leads me beside peaceful streams.
Psalm 23:2

Those who live in the shelter of the Most High will find rest in the shadow of the Almighty. Psalm 91:1

Celebration

Let all who take refuge in you rejoice; let them sing joyful praises forever. Spread your protection over them, that all who love your name may be filled with joy. PSALM 5:11

What causes God to celebrate?

The master said, "Well done, my good and faithful servant. You have been faithful in handling this small amount, so now I will give you many more responsibilities. Let's celebrate together!" Matthew 25:23

In the same way, there is joy in the presence of God's angels when even one sinner repents. Luke 15:10

God celebrates the defeat of sin and evil, the salvation of the lost, and the daily joys and successes of his people. He celebrates when his people faithfully follow and obey his commands.

Regardless of my personal circumstances, what can I always celebrate?

Praise the LORD, for the LORD is good; celebrate his lovely name with music. Psalm 135:3

Sing for joy, O heavens! Rejoice, O earth! Burst into song, O mountains! For the LORD has comforted his people and will have compassion on them in their suffering. Isaiah 49:13

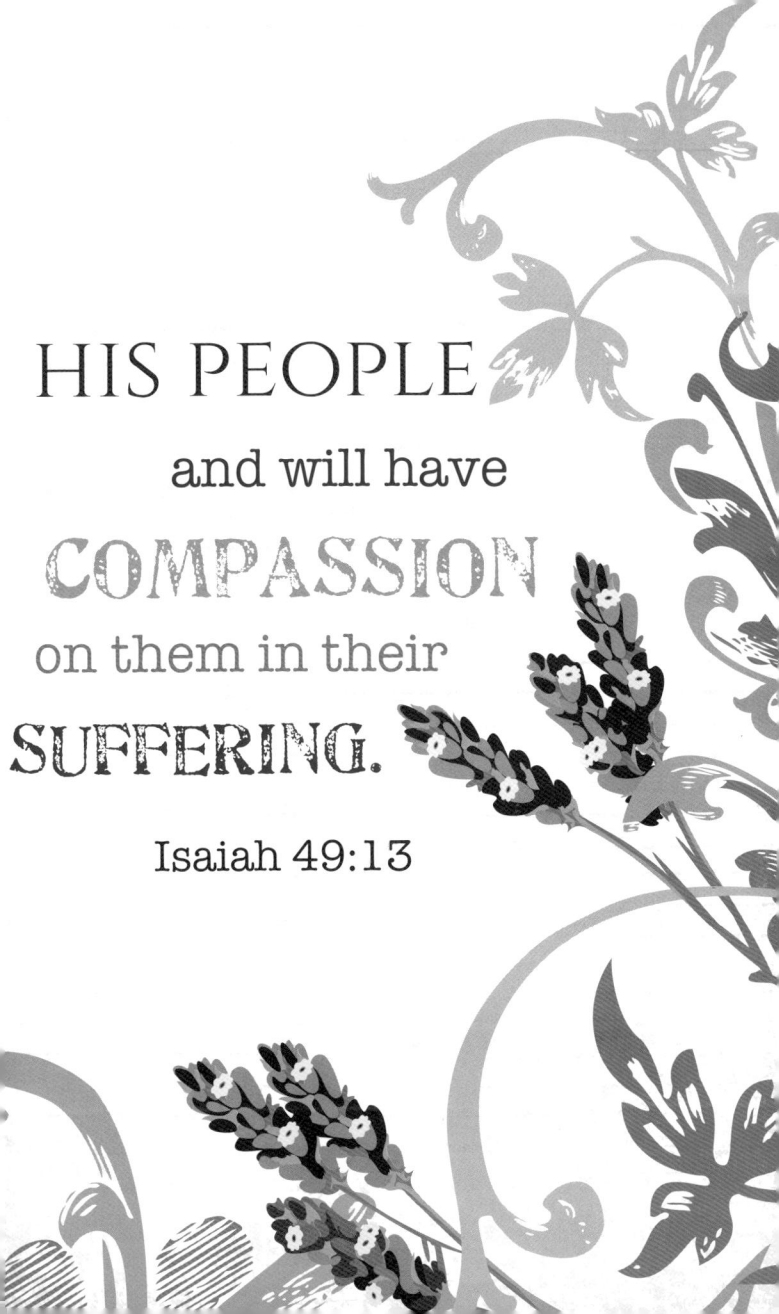

Change

The grass withers and the flowers fade, but the word of our God stands forever. ISAIAH 40:8

How do I change the areas in my life that need to be changed?

Don't copy the behavior and customs of this world, but let God transform you into a new person by changing the way you think. Then you will learn to know God's will for you, which is good and pleasing and perfect. Romans 12:2

Anyone who belongs to Christ has become a new person. The old life is gone; a new life has begun! 2 Corinthians 5:17

Put on your new nature, and be renewed as you learn to know your Creator and become like him. Colossians 3:10

Does God ever change?

I am the Lord, and I do not change. Malachi 3:6

Jesus Christ is the same yesterday, today, and forever. Hebrews 13:8

Lord, you remain the same forever! Your throne continues from generation to generation. Lamentations 5:19

Christlikeness

The Holy Spirit produces this kind of fruit in our lives: love, joy, peace, patience, kindness, goodness, faithfulness, gentleness, and self-control. GALATIANS 5:22-23

What is meant by "Christlikeness"?

[Jesus] said to the crowd, "If any of you wants to be my follower, you must turn from your selfish ways, take up your cross daily, and follow me." Luke 9:23

You must be compassionate, just as your Father is compassionate. Luke 6:36

Since I, your Lord and Teacher, have washed your feet, you ought to wash each other's feet. I have given you an example to follow. Do as I have done to you. John 13:14-15

How do I become like Christ?

All of us who [believe in Christ] can see and reflect the glory of the Lord. And the Lord – who is the Spirit – makes us more and more like him as we are changed into his glorious image.
2 Corinthians 3:18

God, who began the good work within you, will continue his work until it is finally finished on the day when Christ Jesus returns. Philippians 1:6

Church

[Jesus said,] "I will build my church, and all the powers of hell will not conquer it." MATTHEW 16:18

What is the purpose of the church? Why should I attend?

Don't you realize that all of you together are the temple of God and that the Spirit of God lives in you? God will destroy anyone who destroys this temple. For God's temple is holy, and you are that temple.
1 Corinthians 3:16-17

These are the gifts Christ gave to the church: the apostles, the prophets, the evangelists, and the pastors and teachers. Their responsibility is to equip God's people to do his work and build up the church, the body of Christ.   Ephesians 4:11-12

The human body has many parts, but the many parts make up one whole body. So it is with the body of Christ. Some of us are Jews, some are Gentiles, some are slaves, and some are free. But we have all been baptized into one body by one Spirit, and we all share the same Spirit.
1 Corinthians 12:12-13

All believers together form God's family, but only by meeting together can you bond. When you meet together, you can build one another up and help one another.

Comfort

The LORD is good to everyone. He showers compassion on all his creation. PSALM 145:9

How does God comfort me?

When doubts filled my mind, your comfort gave me renewed hope and cheer. Psalm 94:19

Your promise revives me; it comforts me in all my troubles ... I meditate on your age-old regulations; O LORD, they comfort me. Psalm 119:50, 52

He heals the brokenhearted and bandages their wounds. Psalm 147:3

The LORD is compassionate and merciful, slow to get angry and filled with unfailing love. Psalm 103:8

How can I comfort others?

Your love has given me much joy and comfort, my brother, for your kindness has often refreshed the hearts of God's people. Philemon 1:7

All praise to God, the Father of our Lord Jesus Christ. God is our merciful Father and the source of all comfort. He comforts us in all our troubles so that we can comfort others. When they are troubled, we will be able to give them the same comfort God has given us.
2 Corinthians 1:3-4

Remember the ways God has comforted you, and model that same comfort to others. When you have experienced God's assuring love, his guiding wisdom, and his sustaining power, you are able to comfort others with understanding.

Complaining

Let everything you say be good and helpful, so that your words will be an encouragement to those who hear them. EPHESIANS 4:29

What are the dangers of complaining?

Don't speak evil against each other, dear brothers and sisters. If you criticize and judge each other, then you are criticizing and judging God's law. But your job is to obey the law, not to judge whether it applies to you. James 4:11

Don't grumble about each other, brothers and sisters, or you will be judged. For look – the Judge is standing at the door! James 5:9

Complaining about others is indirectly complaining about God and his Word.

What should I do instead of complaining?

Do everything without complaining and arguing, so that no one can criticize you. Live ... as children of God, shining like bright lights in a world full of crooked and perverse people. Philippians 2:14-15

Do not judge others, and you will not be judged. Do not condemn others, or it will all come back against you. Forgive others, and you will be forgiven. Instead of complaining about the weaknesses of others, forgive them as you would like to be forgiven. Luke 6:37

Compromise

You will be successful if you carefully obey the decrees and regulations that the LORD gave to Israel through Moses. Be strong and courageous; do not be afraid or lose heart! 1 CHRONICLES 22:13

When is compromise inappropriate?

Do not let sin control the way you live; do not give in to sinful desires. Romans 6:12

You must not follow the crowd in doing wrong. Exodus 23:2

Dear friend, don't let this bad example influence you. Follow only what is good. 3 John 1:11

How do I live in today's culture without compromising my convictions?

Be very careful never to make a treaty with the people who live in the land where you are going. If you do, you will follow their evil ways and be trapped. Exodus 34:12

Be careful then, dear brothers and sisters. Make sure that your own hearts are not evil and unbelieving, turning you away from the living God. You must warn each other every day, while it is still "today," so that none of you will be deceived by sin and hardened against God. Hebrews 3:12-13

You must always be on the alert when living or working with those who don't see sin as something wrong. You can easily find yourself compromising and agreeing to commit "little" sins.

Conflict

God blesses those who work for peace, for they will be called the children of God. MATTHEW 5:9

What causes conflict?

Pride leads to conflict. Proverbs 13:10

What is causing the quarrels and fights among you? Don't they come from the evil desires at war within you? James 4:1

I love God's law with all my heart. But there is another power within me that is at war with my mind. This power makes me a slave to the sin that is still within me. Romans 7:22-23

How do I keep conflict with others to a minimum?

Do all that you can to live in peace with everyone. Romans 12:18

Make every effort to keep yourselves united in the Spirit, binding yourselves together with peace. Ephesians 4:3

Interfering in someone else's argument is as foolish as yanking a dog's ears. Proverbs 26:17

Confrontation

Gently instruct those who oppose the truth.
Perhaps God will change those people's hearts,
and they will learn the truth. 2 TIMOTHY 2:25

How do I effectively confront others?

If another believer sins, rebuke that person; then if there is repentance, forgive. Luke 17:3

An open rebuke is better than hidden love! Proverbs 27:5

A servant of the Lord must not quarrel but must be kind to everyone, be able to teach, and be patient with difficult people. Gently instruct those who oppose the truth. Perhaps God will change those people's hearts, and they will learn the truth. 2 Timothy 2:24-25

If you punish a mocker, the simpleminded will learn a lesson; if you correct the wise, they will be all the wiser. Proverbs 19:25

An honest answer is like a kiss of friendship. Proverbs 24:26

Confront in private, without quarreling and anger. Approach gently, with kindness and patience. Then let God change their hearts!

Contentment

[The Lord] satisfies the thirsty and fills the hungry with good things. PSALM 107:9

How can I find contentment, regardless of life's circumstances?

I have learned how to be content with whatever I have. I know how to live on almost nothing or with everything. I have learned the secret of living in every situation, whether it is with a full stomach or empty, with plenty or little. For I can do everything through Christ, who gives me strength.   Philippians 4:11-13

How can I be a source of contentment in my relationships?

There is joy for those who deal justly with others and always do what is right.   Psalm 106:3

Joyful are people of integrity, who follow the instructions of the Lord.   Psalm 119:1

How wonderful and pleasant it is when brothers live together in harmony!   Psalm 133:1

You can treat people justly, conduct yourself in a godly manner, and try to be pleasant.

Crisis

God is our refuge and strength, always
ready to help in times of trouble. PSALM 46:1

How should I respond to crisis?

From the depths of despair, O Lord, I call for your help. Hear my cry, O Lord. Pay attention to my prayer.   Psalm 130:1-2

Have mercy on me, O God, have mercy! I look to you for protection. I will hide beneath the shadow of your wings until the danger passes by.   Psalm 57:1

The Lord is my strength and shield. I trust him with all my heart. He helps me, and my heart is filled with joy. I burst out in songs of thanksgiving.   Psalm 28:7

How can I help others in their times of crisis?

Speak up for those who cannot speak for themselves; ensure justice for those being crushed.   Proverbs 31:8

When I am with those who are weak, I share their weakness, for I want to bring the weak to Christ. Yes, I try to find common ground with everyone, doing everything I can to save some.
1 Corinthians 9:22

Criticism

> Some people make cutting remarks, but the words of the wise bring healing. PROVERBS 12:18

How should I respond to criticism?

A fool is quick-tempered, but a wise person stays calm when insulted. An honest witness tells the truth; a false witness tells lies. Proverbs 12:16-17

Better to be criticized by a wise person than to be praised by a fool. Ecclesiastes 7:5

Be happy when you are insulted for being a Christian, for then the glorious Spirit of God rests upon you. 1 Peter 4:14

If you criticize and judge each other, then you are criticizing and judging God's law. James 4:11

[Love] does not demand its own way. It is not irritable, and it keeps no record of being wronged. 1 Corinthians 13:5

If you are criticized, stay calm, and don't lash back. Measure criticism according to the character of the person who is giving it.

Disappointment

Give your burdens to the LORD,
and he will take care of you. PSALM 55:22

Is there a way to avoid or minimize disappointment in my life?

They cried out to you and were saved. They trusted in you and were never disgraced.   Psalm 22:5

I will boast only in the LORD; let all who are helpless take heart.
Psalm 34:2

As the Scriptures say, "I am placing a cornerstone in Jerusalem, chosen for great honor, and anyone who trusts in him will never be disgraced."
1 Peter 2:6

If you live by the principles of Scripture given by God himself, you will face less disappointment because you will have fewer consequences resulting from sinful actions.

Pay careful attention to your own work, for then you will get the satisfaction of a job well done, and you won't need to compare yourself to anyone else.   Galatians 6:4

The satisfaction of doing right and performing a job well will minimize disappointment.

How should I respond to disappointment?

Let's not get tired of doing what is good. At just the right time we will reap a harvest of blessing if we don't give up.   Galatians 6:9

Discipline

> Joyful are those you discipline, LORD, those you teach with your instructions. PSALM 94:12

What are the benefits of discipline?

Obey your father's commands, and don't neglect your mother's instruction … For their command is a lamp and their instruction a light; their corrective discipline is the way to life. Proverbs 6:20, 23

No discipline is enjoyable while it is happening – it's painful! But afterward there will be a peaceful harvest of right living for those who are trained in this way. Hebrews 12:11

I used to wander off until you disciplined me; but now I closely follow your word. Psalm 119:67

How does God discipline you?

Think about it: Just as a parent disciplines a child, the LORD your God disciplines you for your own good. Deuteronomy 8:5

As you endure this divine discipline, remember that God is treating you as his own children. Who ever heard of a child who is never disciplined by its father? Hebrews 12:7

I know, O LORD, that your regulations are fair; you disciplined me because I needed it. Psalm 119:75

Divorce

> Since they are no longer two but one,
> let no one split apart what God has
> joined together. MATTHEW 19:6

What does the Bible say about divorce?

You cry out, "Why doesn't the LORD accept my worship?" I'll tell you why! Because the LORD witnessed the vows you and your wife made when you were young. But you have been unfaithful to her … Didn't the LORD make you one with your wife? In body and spirit you are his … So guard your heart; remain loyal to the wife of your youth. "For I hate divorce!" says the LORD, the God of Israel. Malachi 2:14-16

Some Pharisees came and tried to trap him with this question: "Should a man be allowed to divorce his wife for just any reason?" Matthew 19:3

As the church submits to Christ, so you wives should submit to your husbands in everything. For husbands, this means love your wives, just as Christ loved the church. He gave up his life for her. Ephesians 5:24-25

God sees divorce as wrong because it is breaking a binding commitment you and your spouse made before him. However, if you are divorced, you do not have to forfeit joy and blessing for the rest of your life. While God clearly lists in the Bible what he considers sin (and divorce is on that list), he also clearly explains how to be forgiven and how to restore your relationship with him, even if your marriage cannot be salvaged.

Emotions

> Guard your heart above all else, for it determines the course of your life. PROVERBS 4:23

How can I best handle my emotions?

Clothe yourself with the presence of the Lord Jesus Christ. And don't let yourself think about ways to indulge your evil desires. Romans 13:14

Let the Spirit renew your thoughts and attitudes. Ephesians 4:23

Letting your sinful nature control your mind leads to death. But letting the Spirit control your mind leads to life and peace. Romans 8:6

I cannot keep from speaking. I must express my anguish. My bitter soul must complain. Job 7:11

Many of the older priests, Levites, and other leaders who had seen the first Temple wept aloud when they saw the new Temple's foundation. The others, however, were shouting for joy. The joyful shouting and weeping mingled together in a loud noise that could be heard far in the distance. Ezra 3:12-13

Keep an open dialogue with the Lord and others you trust so that you are not denying your emotions. Share your feelings with a few godly confidants so they can hold you accountable.

Encouragement

May our Lord Jesus Christ himself and God our Father, who loved us and by his grace gave us eternal comfort and a wonderful hope, comfort you and strengthen you in every good thing you do and say. 2 THESSALONIANS 2:16-17

How does God encourage me?

The Scriptures give us hope and encouragement as we wait patiently for God's promises to be fulfilled. Romans 15:4

As soon as I pray, you answer me; you encourage me by giving me strength. Psalm 138:3

I lie in the dust; revive me by your word ... I weep with sorrow; encourage me by your word. Psalm 119:25, 28

How can I be an encouragement to others?

Don't use foul or abusive language. Let everything you say be good and helpful, so that your words will be an encouragement to those who hear them. Ephesians 4:29

A cheerful look brings joy to the heart. Proverbs 15:30

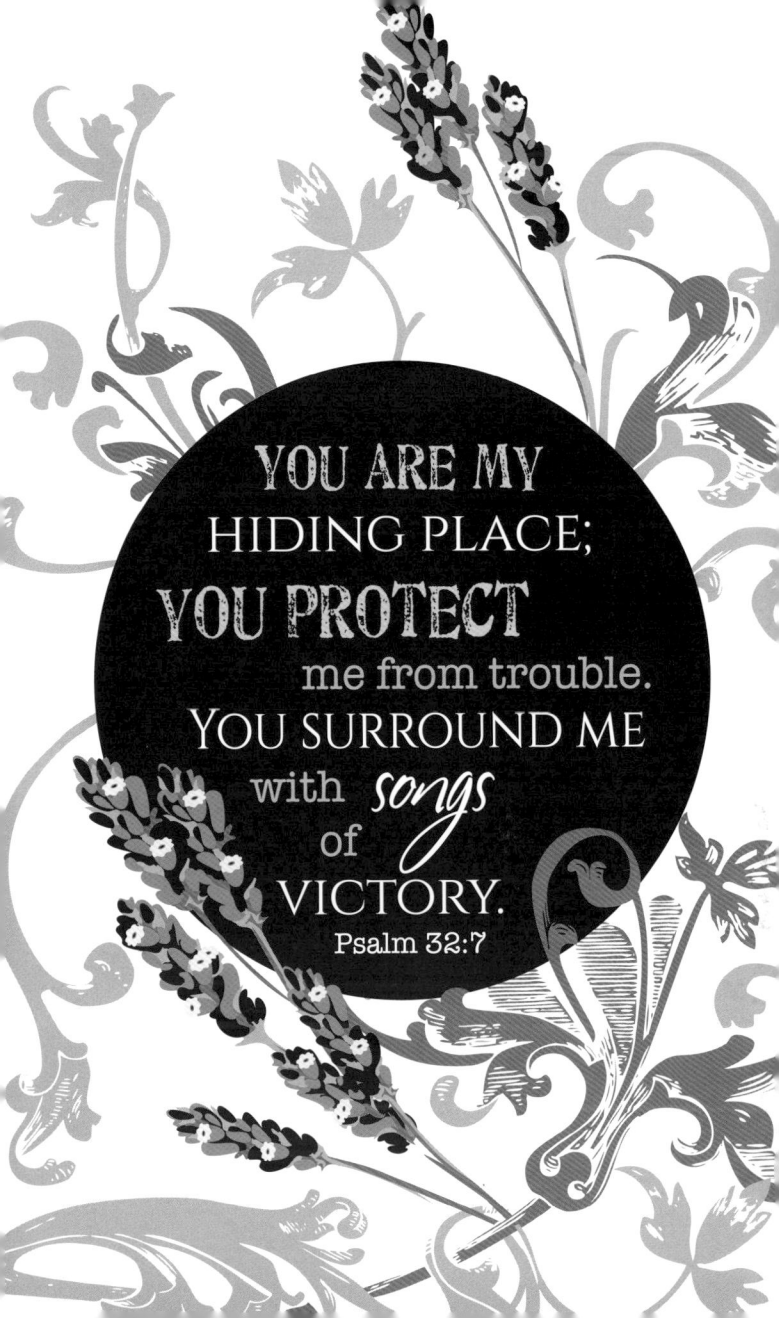

Escape

God has given both his promise and his oath. These two things are unchangeable because it is impossible for God to lie. Therefore, we who have fled to him for refuge can have great confidence as we hold to the hope that lies before us. HEBREWS 6:18

What can I do when I have the desire to escape from my circumstances?

You are my hiding place; you protect me from trouble. You surround me with songs of victory. Psalm 32:7

Have mercy on me, O God, have mercy! I look to you for protection. I will hide beneath the shadow of your wings until the danger passes by. Psalm 57:1

How does God provide ways of escape?

Fear of the Lord is a life-giving fountain; it offers escape from the snares of death. Proverbs 14:27

God is faithful. He will not allow the temptation to be more than you can stand. When you are tempted, he will show you a way out so that you can endure. 1 Corinthians 10:13

Expectations

All praise to God, the Father of our Lord Jesus Christ. It is by his great mercy that we have been born again, because God raised Jesus Christ from the dead. Now we live with great expectation, and we have a priceless inheritance – an inheritance that is kept in heaven for you, pure and undefiled, beyond the reach of change and decay. 1 PETER 1:3-4

What should I expect in life?

The godly can look forward to a reward, while the wicked can expect only judgment. Proverbs 11:23

Shouldn't we expect far greater glory under the new way, now that the Holy Spirit is giving life? ... Since this new way gives us such confidence, we can be very bold. 2 Corinthians 3:8, 12

We can rejoice, too, when we run into problems and trials, for we know that they help us develop endurance. And endurance develops strength of character, and character strengthens our confident hope of salvation. And this hope will not lead to disappointment. For we know how dearly God loves us, because he has given us the Holy Spirit to fill our hearts with his love. Romans 5:3-5

> The LORD directs the steps of the godly.
> He delights in every detail of their lives.
> Though they stumble, they will never fall, for
> the LORD holds them by the hand. PSALM 37:23-24

How do I keep from failing?

God's rest is there for people to enter, but those who first heard this good news failed to enter because they disobeyed God.
Hebrews 4:6

Plans go wrong for lack of advice; many advisers bring success.
Proverbs 15:22

Sin is the cause of many failures. God tells you to live a certain way for a very good reason – to help you make the most of life both now and forever. You will always fail when you go against God's Word and try to live your own way.

When I have failed, how do I get past it and go on?

The godly may trip seven times, but they will get up again. But one disaster is enough to overthrow the wicked. Proverbs 24:16

Though I fall, I will rise again. Though I sit in darkness, the LORD will be my light. Micah 7:8

We are hunted down, but never abandoned by God. We get knocked down, but we are not destroyed. 2 Corinthians 4:9

> When your faith remains strong through many trials, it will bring you much praise and glory and honor on the day when Jesus Christ is revealed to the whole world. 1 PETER 1:7

Why should I have faith in God?

[Jesus said,] "I tell you the truth, those who listen to my message and believe in God who sent me have eternal life." John 5:24

Faith is the confidence that what we hope for will actually happen; it gives us assurance about things we cannot see. Hebrews 11:1

God, with undeserved kindness, declares that we are righteous ... People are made right with God when they believe that Jesus sacrificed his life, shedding his blood. Romans 3:24-25

You will keep in perfect peace all who trust in you, all whose thoughts are fixed on you! Isaiah 26:3

Because of [God's] glory and excellence, he has given us great and precious promises ... In view of all this, make every effort to respond to God's promises. 2 Peter 1:4-5

> The children of your people will live in security. Their children's children will thrive in your presence. PSALM 102:28

What is family? How does the Bible define it?

A man leaves his father and mother and is joined to his wife, and the two are united into one. Genesis 2:24

You are members of God's family. Ephesians 2:19

As for me and my family, we will serve the LORD. Joshua 24:15

My son, obey your father's commands, and don't neglect your mother's instruction … For their command is a lamp and their instruction a light; their corrective discipline is the way to life. Proverbs 6:20, 23

Bring [your children] up with the discipline and instruction that comes from the Lord. Ephesians 6:4

The family is one of God's greatest resources for communicating truth and effecting change in any community. This change is directly related to the family's spiritual commitment and zeal.

> If we confess our sins to him,
> he is faithful and just to forgive
> us our sins and to cleanse us. 1 JOHN 1:9

Do I have to forgive those who hurt me? How many times?

If you forgive those who sin against you, your heavenly Father will forgive you. But if you refuse to forgive others, your Father will not forgive your sins. Matthew 6:14-15

Peter came to [Jesus] and asked, "Lord, how often should I forgive someone who sins against me? Seven times?" "No, not seven times," Jesus replied, "but seventy times seven!" Matthew 18:21-22

When you are praying, first forgive anyone you are holding a grudge against, so that your Father in heaven will forgive your sins, too. Mark 11:25

Make allowance for each other's faults, and forgive anyone who offends you. Remember, the Lord forgave you, so you must forgive others. Colossians 3:13

Just as God forgives you without limit, you should forgive others without counting how many times.

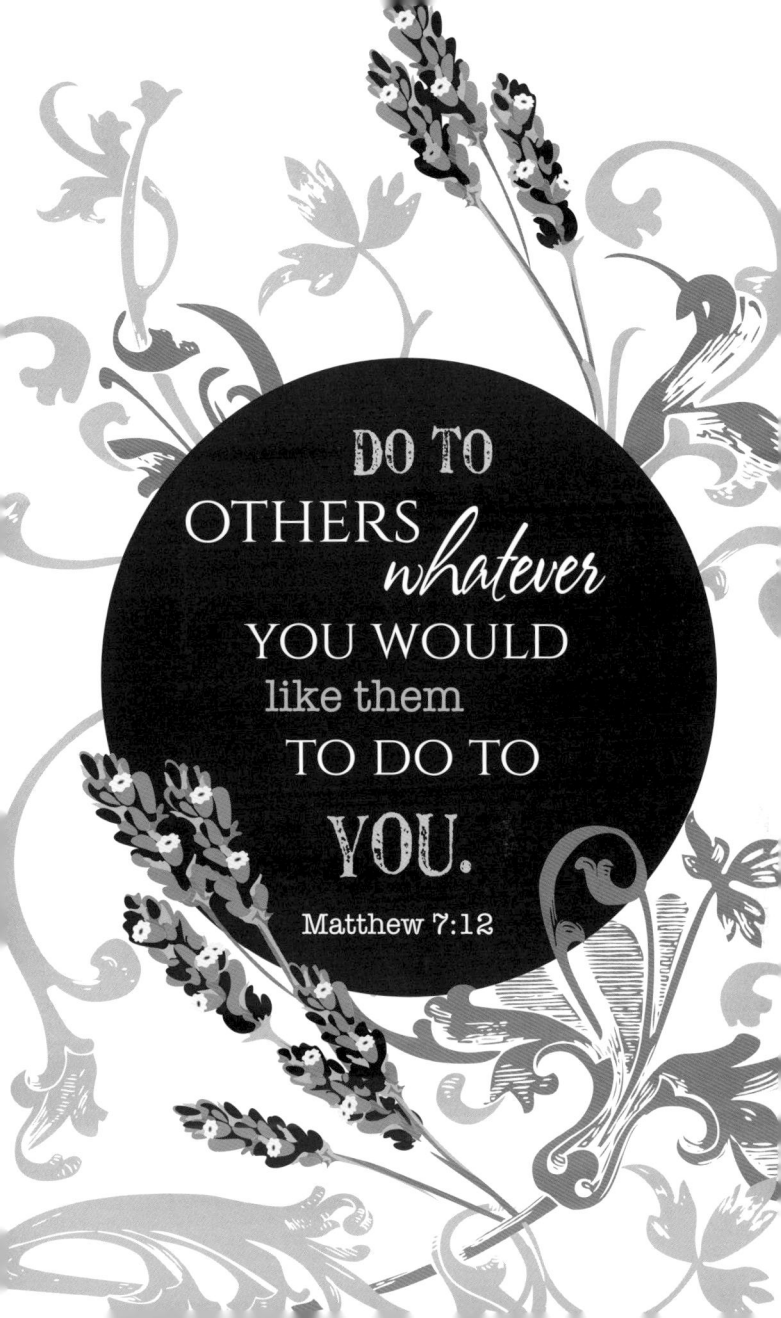

[Jesus said,] "Where two or three gather together as my followers, I am there among them." MATTHEW 18:20

What is the mark of true friendship?

A friend is always loyal, and a brother is born to help in time of need. Proverbs 17:17

Jonathan made a solemn pact with David, because he loved him as he loved himself. 1 Samuel 18:3

Be kind to each other, tenderhearted, forgiving one another, just as God through Christ has forgiven you. Ephesians 4:32

[Jesus said,] "Now you are my friends, since I have told you everything the Father told me." John 15:15

God has said, "I will never fail you. I will never abandon you." Hebrews 13:5

Do to others whatever you would like them to do to you. Matthew 7:12

Remember that God is your constant friend and will never leave you.

Frustration

> Be strong and courageous! Do not be afraid or discouraged. For the Lord your God is with you wherever you go. JOSHUA 1:9

How can I best deal with frustration in my life?

Everything is wearisome beyond description. No matter how much we see, we are never satisfied. No matter how much we hear, we are not content. Ecclesiastes 1:8

Satisfy us each morning with your unfailing love, so we may sing for joy to the end of our lives. Psalm 90:14

You can choose to be joyful in all circumstances by focusing on God rather than what is going on in your life. When you let go and let God work out what is best for you, you will relieve much of your frustration.

What frustrates God?

Oh, how often [the people of Israel] rebelled against [God] in the wilderness and grieved his heart in that dry wasteland. Again and again they tested God's patience and provoked the Holy One of Israel. They did not remember his power and how he rescued them from their enemies. Psalm 78:40-42

"O Israel and Judah, what should I do with you?" asks the Lord. "For your love vanishes like the morning mist and disappears like dew in the sunlight." Hosea 6:4

Gentleness

> He will feed his flock like a shepherd. He will carry the lambs in his arms, holding them close to his heart. He will gently lead the mother sheep with their young. ISAIAH 40:11

How is God gentle?

The LORD is like a father to his children, tender and compassionate to those who fear him. For he knows how weak we are; he remembers we are only dust. Psalm 103:13-14

Jesus said, "Come to me, all of you who are weary and carry heavy burdens, and I will give you rest. Take my yoke upon you. Let me teach you, because I am humble and gentle at heart, and you will find rest for your souls." Matthew 11:28-29

How can I be gentler?

You should clothe yourselves instead with the beauty that comes from within, the unfading beauty of a gentle and quiet spirit, which is so precious to God. 1 Peter 3:4

Since God chose you to be the holy people he loves, you must clothe yourselves with tenderhearted mercy, kindness, humility, gentleness, and patience. Make allowance for each other's faults, and forgive anyone who offends you. Colossians 3:12-13

A gentle answer deflects anger, but harsh words make tempers flare … Gentle words are a tree of life; a deceitful tongue crushes the spirit. Proverbs 15:1, 4

Gossip

If you want to enjoy life and see many happy days, keep your tongue from speaking evil and your lips from telling lies. 1 PETER 3:10

Why is gossip so bad?

Rumors are dainty morsels that sink deep into one's heart.
Proverbs 18:8

Do not spread slanderous gossip among your people. Leviticus 19:16

A gossip goes around telling secrets, but those who are trustworthy can keep a confidence. Proverbs 11:13

Gossip is specifically forbidden by God. It hurts others and destroys your credibility if the gossip proves false.

How do I stop gossip?

Fire goes out without wood, and quarrels disappear when gossip stops.
Proverbs 26:20

Do to others whatever you would like them to do to you.
Matthew 7:12

You must examine the facts carefully. Deuteronomy 13:14

> [The Lord] heals the brokenhearted
> and bandages their wounds. PSALM 147:3

How do I get over my grief?

I will comfort you there in Jerusalem as a mother comforts her child. Isaiah 66:13

All praise to God, the Father of our Lord Jesus Christ. God is our merciful Father and the source of all comfort. 2 Corinthians 1:3

[God] will wipe every tear from their eyes, and there will be no more death or sorrow or crying or pain. Revelation 21:4

For everything there is a season ... A time to cry and a time to laugh. A time to grieve and a time to dance. Ecclesiastes 3:1, 4

The king was overcome with emotion. He went up to the room over the gateway and burst into tears. And as he went, he cried, "O my son Absalom!" 2 Samuel 18:33

Grief is an important part of healing because it allows you to release the emotional pressure of your sorrow. Take time to personally mourn, but also become involved in the steps necessary to bring closure to your loss.

Healing

[The Lord said,] "For you who fear my name, the Sun of Righteousness will rise with healing in his wings. And you will go free, leaping with joy like calves let out to pasture." MALACHI 4:2

How does God heal people?

You have turned my mourning into joyful dancing. Psalm 30:11

"Lord," he said, "if you are willing, you can heal me and make me clean." Jesus reached out and touched him. "I am willing," he said. "Be healed!" Luke 5:12-13

Are any of you sick? You should call for the elders of the church to come and pray over you, anointing you with oil in the name of the Lord. James 5:14

He was pierced for our rebellion, crushed for our sins. He was beaten so we could be whole. He was whipped so we could be healed. Isaiah 53:5

Lord, your discipline is good, for it leads to life and health. Isaiah 38:16

The Lord will guide you continually, giving you water when you are dry and restoring your strength. You will be like a well-watered garden, like an ever-flowing spring. ISAIAH 58:11

How do I keep my soul in good health?

A cheerful heart is good medicine, but a broken spirit saps a person's strength. Proverbs 17:22

Do not waste time arguing over godless ideas and old wives' tales. Instead, train yourself to be godly. "Physical training is good, but training for godliness is much better, promising benefits in this life and in the life to come." 1 Timothy 4:7-8

Spiritual exercise is as purposeful and strenuous as physical exercise. But the benefits of spiritual fitness last for eternity, while the benefits of physical fitness last only as long as your body lasts.

Home

The Lord curses the house of the wicked, but he blesses the home of the upright. PROVERBS 3:33

How can I establish my home the way God wants it?

Unless the Lord builds a house, the work of the builders is wasted. Psalm 127:1

A house is built by wisdom and becomes strong through good sense. Through knowledge its rooms are filled with all sorts of precious riches and valuables. Proverbs 24:3-4

How can I experience God's blessing on my home?

Teach [God's words] to your children. Talk about them when you are at home and when you are on the road, when you are going to bed and when you are getting up. Write them on the doorposts of your house and on your gates. Deuteronomy 11:19-20

The house of the wicked will be destroyed, but the tent of the godly will flourish. Proverbs 14:11

There is treasure in the house of the godly, but the earnings of the wicked bring trouble. Proverbs 15:6

God promises to bless the homes of those who strive to be righteous.

Hope

O Israel, hope in the LORD; for with the LORD there is unfailing love. His redemption overflows. PSALM 130:7

In what or whom do we hope?

Lord, where do I put my hope? My only hope is in you. Psalm 39:7

You place your hope in the Lord himself, because he holds you fast today, and he determines your future.

Why should I trust God as my hope?

God has given both his promise and his oath. These two things are unchangeable because it is impossible for God to lie. Therefore, we who have fled to him for refuge can have great confidence as we hold to the hope that lies before us. This hope is a strong and trustworthy anchor for our souls. It leads us through the curtain into God's inner sanctuary. Hebrews 6:18-19

Let us hold tightly without wavering to the hope we affirm, for God can be trusted to keep his promise. Hebrews 10:23

Through Christ you have come to trust in God. And you have placed your faith and hope in God because he raised Christ from the dead and gave him great glory. 1 Peter 1:21

The Scriptures give us hope and encouragement as we wait patiently for God's promises to be fulfilled. Romans 15:4

Hospitality

Don't forget to show hospitality to strangers, for some who have done this have entertained angels without realizing it! HEBREWS 13:2

How should I show hospitality to others?

Cheerfully share your home with those who need a meal or a place to stay. 1 Peter 4:9

The man went home with Laban, and Laban unloaded the camels, gave him straw for their bedding, fed them, and provided water for the man and the camel drivers to wash their feet.
Genesis 24:32

Offering food to eat and providing a place to stay – the basics of good hospitality – are simple acts of kindness that can be offered by almost anyone.

To whom should I be hospitable?

When God's people are in need, be ready to help them. Always be eager to practice hospitality. Romans 12:13

You are being faithful to God when you care for the traveling teachers who pass through, even though they are strangers to you. 3 John 1:5

Share your food with the hungry, and give shelter to the homeless. Give clothes to those who need them, and do not hide from relatives who need your help. Isaiah 58:7

Humility

> Those who exalt themselves will be humbled, and those who humble themselves will be exalted. MATTHEW 23:12

What is true humility?

Those who are left will be the lowly and humble, for it is they who trust in the name of the Lord. Zephaniah 3:12

Anyone who becomes as humble as this little child is the greatest in the Kingdom of Heaven. Matthew 18:4

How was Jesus humble?

Rejoice, O people of Zion! Shout in triumph, O people of Jerusalem! Look, your king is coming to you. He is righteous and victorious, yet he is humble, riding on a donkey – riding on a donkey's colt. Zechariah 9:9

You must have the same attitude that Christ Jesus had. Though he was God, he did not think of equality with God as something to cling to. Instead, he gave up his divine privileges; he took the humble position of a slave and was born as a human being. When he appeared in human form, he humbled himself in obedience to God and died a criminal's death on a cross. Philippians 2:5-8

Husbands

A worthy wife is a crown for her husband, but a disgraceful woman is like cancer in his bones. PROVERBS 12:4

What are some ways I can meet my husband's needs?

This is how the holy women of old made themselves beautiful. They trusted God and accepted the authority of their husbands. 1 Peter 3:5

Her husband can trust her, and she will greatly enrich his life. Proverbs 31:11

A married woman has to think about her earthly responsibilities and how to please her husband. 1 Corinthians 7:34

How can I best help my husband if he does not know Jesus Christ as his Savior and Lord?

You wives must accept the authority of your husbands. Then, even if some refuse to obey the Good News, your godly lives will speak to them without any words. They will be won over by observing your pure and reverent lives. 1 Peter 3:1-2

Godly loving is the best way to witness to an unbelieving mate.

I wait quietly before God, for my victory comes from him ... Let all that I am wait quietly before God, for my hope is in him ... O my people, trust in him at all times. Pour out your heart to him, for God is our refuge. PSALM 62:1, 5, 8

How can I deal with the tensions infertility causes?

Since the world began, no ear has heard and no eye has seen a God like you, who works for those who wait for him! Isaiah 64:4

For reasons you do not fully understand, God does not always allow you to have what you desire. Maybe it's because he has a different plan. Or maybe it is simply because life is dealing a hard blow. But for now, trust that God is in control, he loves you, and he is with you in your heartache.

How can I accept God's timing?

The Lord must wait for you to come to him so he can show you his love and compassion. For the Lord is a faithful God. Blessed are those who wait for his help. Isaiah 30:18

The Lord is good to those who depend on him, to those who search for him. So it is good to wait quietly for salvation from the Lord. Lamentations 3:25-26

Intimacy

If you seek him, you will find him. 1 CHRONICLES 28:9

What is the basis for true and lasting intimacy in marriage?

As the church submits to Christ, so you wives should submit to your husbands ... Husbands ... love your wives, just as Christ loved the church. He gave up his life for her to make her holy and clean ... Husbands ought to love their wives as they love their own bodies. For a man who loves his wife actually shows love for himself. No one hates his own body but feeds and cares for it, just as Christ cares for the church. Ephesians 5:24-26, 28-29

How can I experience an intimate relationship with God?

The LORD is close to all who call on him, yes, to all who call on him in truth. Psalm 145:18

Come close to God, and God will come close to you. Wash your hands, you sinners; purify your hearts, for your loyalty is divided between God and the world. James 4:8

Jesus [said], "'You must love the LORD your God with all your heart, all your soul, and all your mind.'" Matthew 22:37

My heart has heard you say, "Come and talk with me." And my heart responds, "LORD, I am coming." Psalm 27:8

Joy

[Jesus said,] "I have told you these things so that you will be filled with my joy. Yes, your joy will overflow!" JOHN 15:11

Does God promise me joy?

May all who search for you be filled with joy and gladness in you. May those who love your salvation repeatedly shout, "The LORD is great!" Psalm 40:16

Let the godly rejoice. Let them be glad in God's presence. Let them be filled with joy. Psalm 68:3

The Lord himself is the wellspring of true joy. The more you love him, know him, walk with him, and become like him, the greater your joy.

How can I be joyful in the midst of difficult circumstances?

Don't be surprised at the fiery trials you are going through, as if something strange were happening to you. Instead, be very glad – for these trials make you partners with Christ in his suffering, so that you will have the wonderful joy of seeing his glory when it is revealed to all the world. 1 Peter 4:12-13

We confidently and joyfully look forward to sharing God's glory. Romans 5:2

Kindness

If you give even a cup of cold water to one of the least of my followers, you will surely be rewarded. MATTHEW 10:42

Why should I be kind?

Be kind to each other, tenderhearted, forgiving one another, just as God through Christ has forgiven you. Ephesians 4:32

Do to others whatever you would like them to do to you.
Matthew 7:12

You know the generous grace of our Lord Jesus Christ. Though he was rich, yet for your sakes he became poor, so that by his poverty he could make you rich. 2 Corinthians 8:9

Be kind because God has been kind to you and asks you to pass it on to others. It is a way to show others his love. If you expect others to be kind to you, you must be kind to them.

How has God shown kindness to me?

When God our Savior revealed his kindness and love, he saved us, not because of the righteous things we had done, but because of his mercy. Titus 3:4-5

The Lord is merciful and compassionate, slow to get angry and filled with unfailing love ... The Lord is righteous in everything he does; he is filled with kindness.
Psalm 145:8, 17

Come and listen to my counsel. I'll share my
heart with you and make you wise. PROVERBS 1:23

Does God really listen when I pray?

He will listen to the prayers of the destitute. He will not reject their pleas. Psalm 102:17

We are confident that he hears us whenever we ask for anything that pleases him. And since we know he hears us when we make our requests, we also know that he will give us what we ask for.
1 John 5:14-15

How can I better listen to God?

Listen to my voice in the morning, LORD. Each morning I bring my requests to you and wait expectantly.   Psalm 5:3

Come to God regularly, and wait expectantly. God always answers. Wait patiently!

Be still, and know that I am God! Psalm 46:10

After the earthquake there was a fire, but the LORD was not in the fire. And after the fire there was the sound of a gentle whisper.
1 Kings 19:12

Recognize that God's power and greatness are often displayed in quietness and gentleness.

Loneliness

Even when I walk through the darkest valley, I will not be afraid, for you are close beside me. Your rod and your staff protect and comfort me. PSALM 23:4

Why does God allow me to be lonely?

The LORD God said, "It is not good for the man to be alone. I will make a helper who is just right for him." Genesis 2:18

Nothing can ever separate us from God's love. Neither death nor life, neither angels nor demons, neither our fears for today nor our worries about tomorrow – not even the powers of hell can separate us from God's love. No power in the sky above or in the earth below – indeed, nothing in all creation will ever be able to separate us from the love of God that is revealed in Christ Jesus our Lord. Romans 8:38-39

God did not intend for you to be lonely. Quite the contrary, it was God who recognized Adam's need for companionship. It was then that God created woman (see Genesis 2:19-22). God also promised he will always be there for you. Nothing can separate you from him.

How can I avoid loneliness?

We are many parts of one body, and we all belong to each other.
Romans 12:5

Let us not neglect our meeting together, as some people do, but encourage one another, especially now that the day of his return is drawing near.
Hebrews 10:25

Loss

The LORD is close to the brokenhearted; he rescues those whose spirits are crushed. PSALM 34:18

How do I deal with loss in my life?

You suffered along with those who were thrown into jail, and when all you owned was taken from you, you accepted it with joy. You knew there were better things waiting for you that will last forever. Hebrews 10:34

By not denying your loss and allowing yourself to grieve. By serving God and others with all the energy and enthusiasm you can muster, you will begin to find healing. And as a Christian, you have the comfort of knowing that one day you will be with God in heaven, where all grief will be gone forever.

How can God help me survive life's losses?

LORD, you know the hopes of the helpless. Surely you will hear their cries and comfort them. Psalm 10:17

You have turned my mourning into joyful dancing. You have taken away my clothes of mourning and clothed me with joy, that I might sing praises to you and not be silent. O LORD my God, I will give you thanks forever! Psalm 30:11-12

God blesses those who mourn, for they will be comforted. Matthew 5:4

All praise to God, the Father of our Lord Jesus Christ. God is our merciful Father and the source of all comfort. 2 Corinthians 1:3

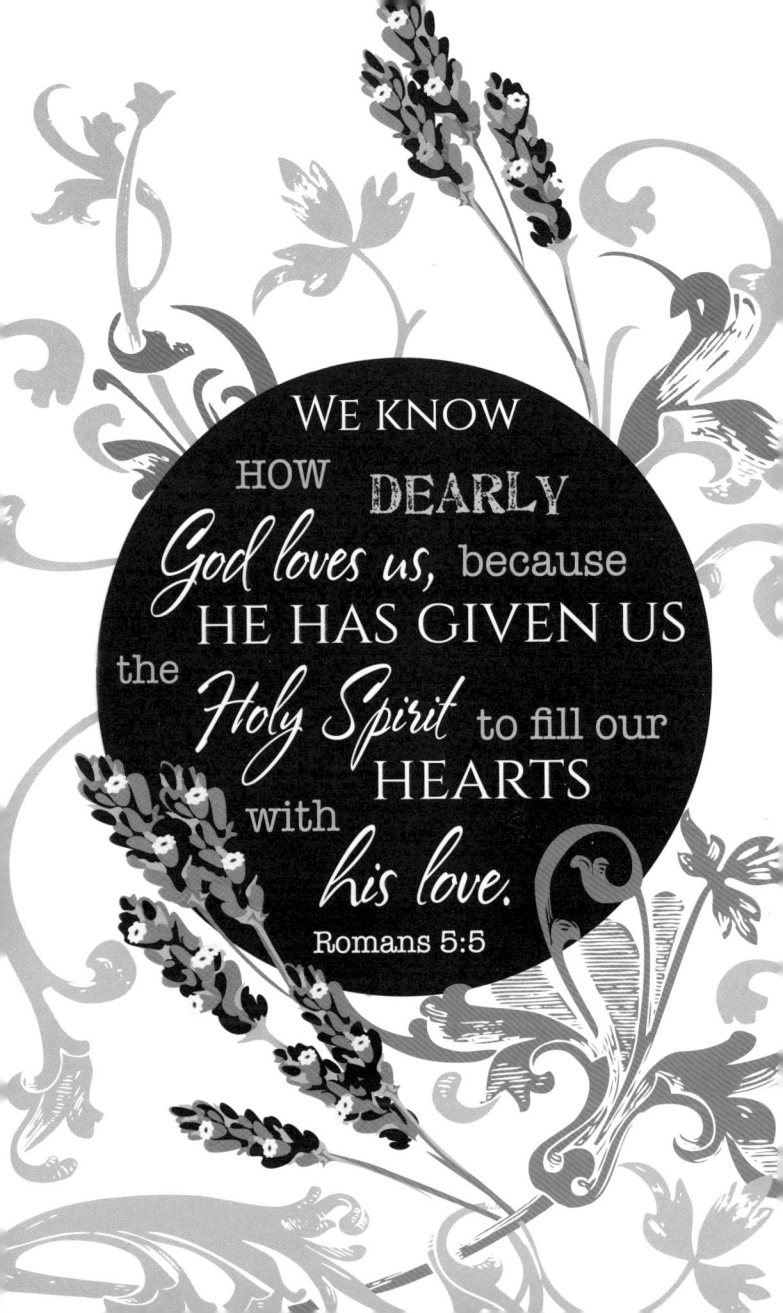

Love

God loved the world so much that he gave his one and only Son, so that everyone who believes in him will not perish but have eternal life. JOHN 3:16

Must I love other people?

[Jesus said,] "I am giving you a new commandment: Love each other. Just as I have loved you, you should love each other. Your love for one another will prove to the world that you are my disciples." John 13:34-35

No one has ever seen God. But if we love each other, God lives in us, and his love is brought to full expression in us. 1 John 4:12

Most important of all, continue to show deep love for each other, for love covers a multitude of sins. 1 Peter 4:8

How can I know that God loves me?

We know how dearly God loves us, because he has given us the Holy Spirit to fill our hearts with his love. Romans 5:5

God showed how much he loved us by sending his one and only Son into the world so that we might have eternal life through him. This is real love. 1 John 4:9-10

A man leaves his father and mother and is joined to his wife, and the two are united into one. EPHESIANS 5:31

What kind of relationship should a marriage be?

The LORD God said, "It is not good for the man to be alone. I will make a helper who is just right for him." Genesis 2:18

Two people are better off than one, for they can help each other succeed. If one person falls, the other can reach out and help. But someone who falls alone is in real trouble. Ecclesiastes 4:9-10

The head of every man is Christ, the head of woman is man, and the head of Christ is God. 1 Corinthians 11:3

The man who finds a wife finds a treasure, and he receives favor from the LORD. Proverbs 18:22

Submit to your husbands as to the Lord. For a husband is the head of his wife as Christ is the head of the church. He is the Savior of his body, the church. As the church submits to Christ, so you wives should submit to your husbands in everything. Ephesians 5:22-24

Marriage at its best is a relationship so close and intimate that the two of you work together as one. It involves mutual trust, support, defense, comfort, productivity, vulnerability, and responsibility.

Think about what I am saying. The Lord will help you understand all these things. 2 TIMOTHY 2:7

How do I meditate?

I wait quietly before God, for my victory comes from him ... Let all that I am wait quietly before God, for my hope is in him. Psalm 62:1, 5

[The godly] delight in the law of the LORD, meditating on it day and night. Psalm 1:2

Meditation involves thinking about God quietly and intently, with confidence that he will hear you and you will hear him. It involves taking the time to read God's Word and consider it. He often speaks to your heart as you read the words he has written for you.

What should I think about when I meditate?

I recall all you have done, O LORD; I remember your wonderful deeds of long ago. They are constantly in my thoughts. I cannot stop thinking about your mighty works. Psalm 77:11-12

Fix your thoughts on what is true, and honorable, and right, and pure, and lovely, and admirable. Think about things that are excellent and worthy of praise. Philippians 4:8

Oh, how I love your instructions! I think about them all day long. Psalm 119:97

Mercy

The LORD is compassionate and merciful, slow to get angry and filled with unfailing love. PSALM 103:8

What is mercy?

In all their suffering he also suffered, and he personally rescued them. In his love and mercy he redeemed them. He lifted them up and carried them through all the years. Isaiah 63:9

The faithful love of the LORD never ends! His mercies never cease. Lamentations 3:22

Where is another God like you, who pardons the guilt of the remnant, overlooking the sins of his special people? You will not stay angry with your people forever, because you delight in showing unfailing love. Micah 7:18

Mercy is more than exemption from the punishment you deserve for your sins: It is receiving the undeserved gift of salvation as well. Mercy is experiencing favor with almighty God through his forgiveness.

How can I show mercy?

Since God chose you to be the holy people he loves, you must clothe yourselves with tenderhearted mercy, kindness, humility, gentleness, and patience. Colossians 3:12

The LORD has told you what is good, and this is what he requires of you: to do what is right, to love mercy, and to walk humbly with your God. Micah 6:8

Mistakes

I focus on this one thing: Forgetting the past and looking forward to what lies ahead, I press on to reach the end of the race and receive the heavenly prize for which God, through Christ Jesus, is calling us. PHILIPPIANS 3:13-14

How can I learn from my mistakes?

"Why are you so angry?" the LORD asked Cain. "Why do you look so dejected? You will be accepted if you do what is right. But if you refuse to do what is right, then watch out! Sin is crouching at the door, eager to control you. But you must subdue it and be its master." Genesis 4:6-7

Whoever stubbornly refuses to accept criticism will suddenly be destroyed beyond recovery. Proverbs 29:1

Indeed, we all make many mistakes. For if we could control our tongues, we would be perfect and could also control ourselves in every other way. James 3:2

When you are told you have made a mistake, respond with humility. Consider the source and the substance of the criticism, then listen and learn for the future.

modesty

> Charm is deceptive, and beauty does not last; but a woman who fears the LORD will be greatly praised. PROVERBS 31:30

What is the importance of modesty?

Don't you realize that your body is the temple of the Holy Spirit, who lives in you and was given to you by God? You do not belong to yourself, for God bought you with a high price. So you must honor God with your body. 1 Corinthians 6:19-20

Don't be concerned about the outward beauty of fancy hairstyles, expensive jewelry, or beautiful clothes. You should clothe yourselves instead with the beauty that comes from within, the unfading beauty of a gentle and quiet spirit, which is so precious to God. 1 Peter 3:3-4

How should I show modesty in my behavior?

Because we belong to the day, we must live decent lives for all to see. Romans 13:13

Once you were full of darkness, but now you have light from the Lord. So live as people of light! Ephesians 5:8

We are instructed to turn from godless living and sinful pleasures. We should live in this evil world with wisdom, righteousness, and devotion to God. Titus 2:12

Don't worry about these things, saying, "What will we eat? What will we drink? What will we wear?" These things dominate the thoughts of unbelievers, but your heavenly Father already knows all your needs. Seek the Kingdom of God above all else, and live righteously, and he will give you everything you need. MATTHEW 6:31-33

What is a proper attitude toward money?

No one can serve two masters ... You cannot serve both God and money. Matthew 6:24

The love of money is the root of all kinds of evil. 1 Timothy 6:10

I have learned how to be content with whatever I have ... I have learned the secret of living in every situation, whether it is with a full stomach or empty, with plenty or little. Philippians 4:11-12

This same God who takes care of me will supply all your needs from his glorious riches, which have been given to us in Christ Jesus. Philippians 4:19

How can I best handle my money?

"Bring all the tithes into the storehouse ... If you do," says the LORD of Heaven's Armies, "I will open the windows of heaven for you. I will pour out a blessing so great you won't have enough room to take it in! Try it! Put me to the test!" Malachi 3:10

Mothers

> Honor your father and mother. Then you will live a long, full life in the land the LORD your God is giving you. EXODUS 20:12

What qualities should a mother possess?

A wise woman builds her home, but a foolish woman tears it down with her own hands. Proverbs 14:1

It was by faith that Moses' parents hid him for three months when he was born. They saw that God had given them an unusual child, and they were not afraid to disobey the king's command. Hebrews 11:23

A godly mother exercises great faith on behalf of her children.

What are some of the responsibilities of a mother?

I, too, was once my father's son, tenderly loved as my mother's only child. Proverbs 4:3

Just as a parent disciplines a child, the LORD your God disciplines you for your own good. Deuteronomy 8:5

My child, … don't neglect your mother's instruction. Proverbs 1:8

A mother should love her children tenderly and discipline them with the same loving hand the Lord shows to her. A mother should teach her children God's ways.

Motives

> If you plan to do evil, you will be lost; if you plan to do good, you will receive unfailing love and faithfulness. PROVERBS 14:22

How can I have purer motives?

May the words of my mouth and the meditation of my heart be pleasing to you, O Lord, my rock and my redeemer.   Psalm 19:14

Start by asking God to change the way you think by changing your heart.

Fire tests the purity of silver and gold, but the Lord tests the heart.   Proverbs 17:3

My conscience is clear, but that doesn't prove I'm right. It is the Lord himself who will examine me and decide.   1 Corinthians 4:4

Put me on trial, Lord, and cross-examine me. Test my motives and my heart. Psalm 26:2

Remember that God alone knows your heart. Ask him to reveal to you any area in which your motives are less than pure. Welcome it when God tests your motives. This gives you an opportunity to grow.

> This same God who takes care of me will supply all your needs from his glorious riches, which have been given to us in Christ Jesus. PHILIPPIANS 4:19

Does God really care about my daily needs?

I will be your God throughout your lifetime – until your hair is white with age. I made you, and I will care for you. I will carry you along and save you. Isaiah 46:4

Look at the birds. They don't plant or harvest or store food in barns, for your heavenly Father feeds them. And aren't you far more valuable to him than they are? Matthew 6:26

God will generously provide all you need. Then you will always have everything you need and plenty left over to share with others. 2 Corinthians 9:8

What do I really need?

Let us come boldly to the throne of our gracious God. There we will receive his mercy, and we will find grace to help us when we need it most. Hebrews 4:16

Patient endurance is what you need now, so that you will continue to do God's will. Then you will receive all that he has promised. Hebrews 10:36

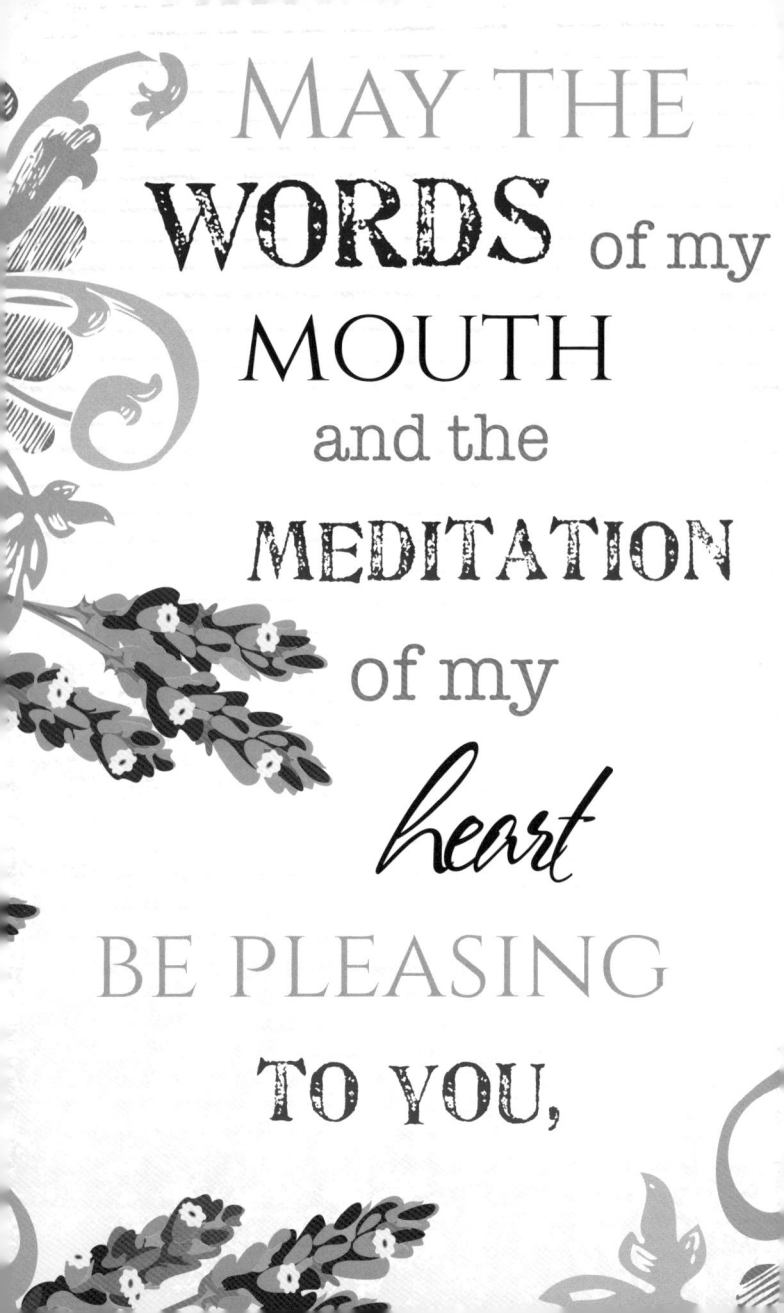

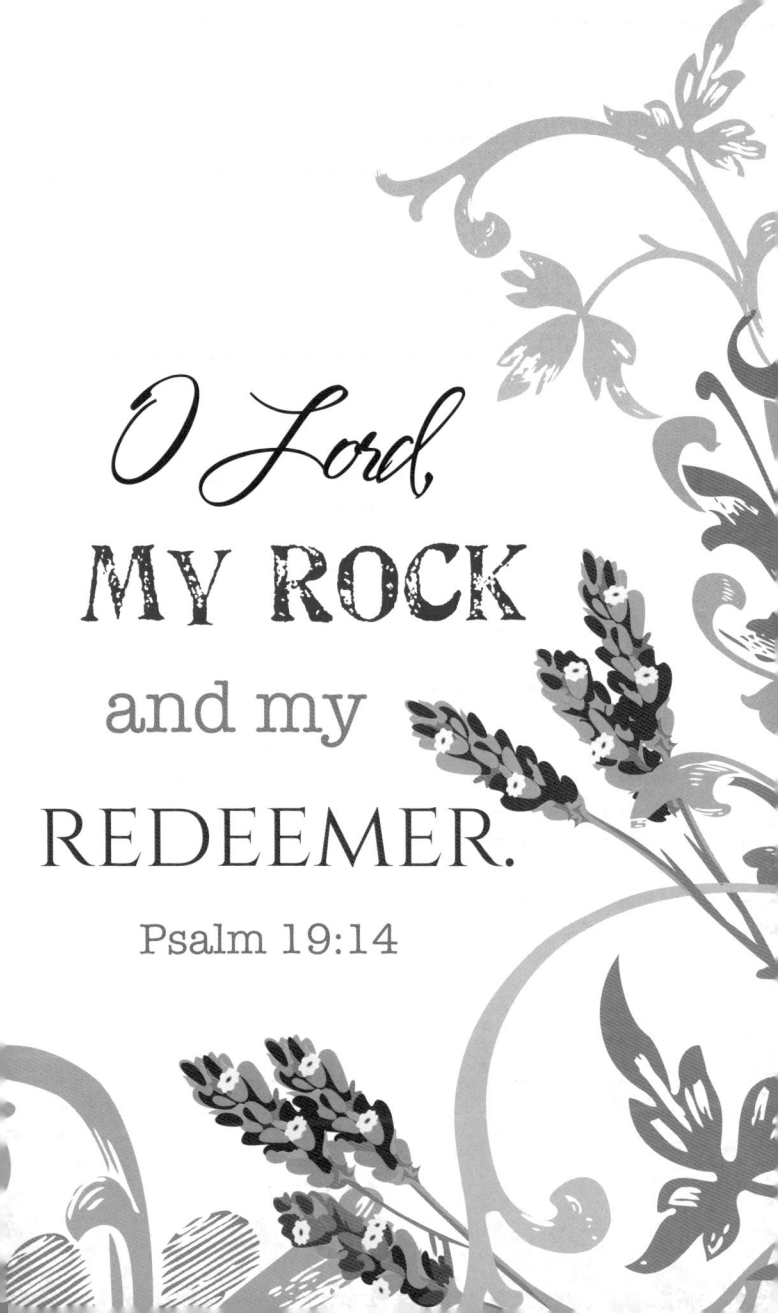

Yes indeed, it is good when you obey
the royal law as found in the Scriptures:
"Love your neighbor as yourself." JAMES 2:8

What are my responsibilities to my neighbor?

The whole law can be summed up in this one command: "Love your neighbor as yourself." Galatians 5:14

If you can help your neighbor now, don't say, "Come back tomorrow, and then I'll help you." Proverbs 3:28

The commandments say, "You must not commit adultery. You must not murder. You must not steal. You must not covet." These – and other such commandments – are summed up in this one commandment: "Love your neighbor as yourself." Love does no wrong to others, so love fulfills the requirements of God's law. Romans 13:9-10

You must not testify falsely against your neighbor. Exodus 20:16

Be careful to live properly among your unbelieving neighbors. Then even if they accuse you of doing wrong, they will see your honorable behavior, and they will give honor to God when he judges the world. 1 Peter 2:12

Obedience

[The Lord said,] "If you will obey me and keep my covenant, you will be my own special treasure from among all the peoples on earth; for all the earth belongs to me." EXODUS 19:5

Is obedience to God really necessary, since I am saved by faith?

What does the Lord your God require of you? He requires only that you fear the Lord your God, and live in a way that pleases him, and love him and serve him with all your heart and soul. And you must always obey the Lord's commands and decrees … for your own good. Deuteronomy 10:12-13

Obey me, and I will be your God, and you will be my people. Jeremiah 7:23

In what ways does God want me to obey him?

You must be careful to obey all the commands of the Lord your God, following his instructions in every detail. Deuteronomy 5:32

What is more pleasing to the Lord: your burnt offerings and sacrifices or your obedience to his voice? Listen! Obedience is better than sacrifice, and submission is better than offering the fat of rams. 1 Samuel 15:22

Parenting

Direct your children onto the right path, and when they are older, they will not leave it. PROVERBS 22:6

What does the Bible say about the role of parents?

The LORD corrects those he loves, just as a father corrects a child in whom he delights. Proverbs 3:12

No discipline is enjoyable while it is happening – it's painful! But afterward there will be a peaceful harvest of right living for those who are trained in this way. Hebrews 12:11

Parents are to discipline their children with consistency, wisdom, and love.

How can I most effectively teach my child about God and his ways?

Commit yourselves wholeheartedly to these words of mine. Tie them to your hands and wear them on your forehead as reminders. Teach them to your children. Talk about them when you are at home and when you are on the road, when you are going to bed and when you are getting up. Deuteronomy 11:18-19

As a parent, you have the remarkable privilege of living what you want your children to learn, sharing God's truth with them, guiding them in the right way to go, and then watching with joy as your work continues in future generations.

Patience

The Lord is a faithful God. Blessed are those who wait for his help. ISAIAH 30:18

How can I develop more patience?

I waited patiently for the Lord to help me, and he turned to me and heard my cry. Psalm 40:1

If it seems slow in coming, wait patiently, for it will surely take place. It will not be delayed. Habakkuk 2:3

The Holy Spirit produces this kind of fruit in our lives: love, joy, peace, patience. Galatians 5:22

If we look forward to something we don't yet have, we must wait patiently and confidently. Romans 8:25

Rejoice in our confident hope. Be patient in trouble, and keep on praying. Romans 12:12

If God is going to do what is best for you, then his plan for you will be accomplished on his schedule, not yours. Keeping that in mind, you can actually become excited about waiting for him to act, anticipating the good things he will work in your life.

Poverty

> Oh, the joys of those who are kind to the poor! The LORD rescues them when they are in trouble. PSALM 41:1

Doesn't God care that I'm poor? I feel so lonely when I realize that so many others seem to have all they need, and I'm struggling.

You are a tower of refuge to the poor, O LORD, a tower of refuge to the needy in distress. You are a refuge from the storm and a shelter from the heat. Isaiah 25:4

Does it mean he no longer loves us if we have trouble or calamity, or are persecuted, or hungry, or destitute, or in danger, or threatened with death? … No, despite all these things, overwhelming victory is ours through Christ, who loved us. Romans 8:35, 37

Don't love money; be satisfied with what you have. For God has said, "I will never fail you. I will never abandon you." Hebrews 13:5

Does God really care about the poor?

He will rescue the poor when they cry to him; he will help the oppressed, who have no one to defend them. Psalm 72:12

Feed the hungry, and help those in trouble. Then your light will shine out from the darkness, and the darkness around you will be as bright as noon. Isaiah 58:10

Praise

> Praise the LORD, for he has shown me the wonders of his unfailing love. PSALM 31:21

Why is it so important to praise God?

Great is the LORD! He is most worthy of praise! He is to be feared above all gods. The gods of other nations are mere idols, but the LORD made the heavens! 1 Chronicles 16:25-26

All heaven will praise your great wonders, LORD; myriads of angels will praise you for your faithfulness. Psalm 89:5

Who can list the glorious miracles of the LORD? Who can ever praise him enough? Psalm 106:2

How can I express praise to God?

With all my heart I will praise you, O Lord my God. I will give glory to your name forever. Psalm 86:12

Each morning and evening they stood before the LORD to sing songs of thanks and praise to him. 1 Chronicles 23:30

I will praise the LORD at all times. I will constantly speak his praises. Psalm 34:1

Praise the LORD! Sing to the LORD a new song. Sing his praises in the assembly of the faithful. Psalm 149:1

Prayer

[The Lord said,] "If my people who are called by my name will humble themselves and pray and seek my face and turn from their wicked ways, I will hear from heaven and will forgive their sins." 2 CHRONICLES 7:14

What is prayer?

The Lord is close to all who call on him, yes, to all who call on him in truth. Psalm 145:18

Prayer is conversation with God. It is simply talking with God and listening to him, honestly telling him your thoughts and feelings, praising him, thanking him, confessing sin, and asking for his help and advice.

Does the Bible teach a "right" way to pray?

Pray in the Spirit at all times and on every occasion. Stay alert and be persistent in your prayers for all believers everywhere. Ephesians 6:18

[Jesus said,] "Pray like this: Our Father in heaven, may your name be kept holy. May your Kingdom come soon. May your will be done on earth, as it is in heaven. Give us today the food we need, and forgive us our sins, as we have forgiven those who sin against us. And don't let us yield to temptation, but rescue us from the evil one." Matthew 6:9-13

Confess your sins to each other and pray for each other so that you may be healed. The earnest prayer of a righteous person has great power and produces wonderful results. James 5:16

Priorities

Seek the Kingdom of God above all else ... and he will give you everything you need. MATTHEW 6:33

What should be my highest priority?

Jesus [said], "The most important commandment is this: 'Listen, O Israel! The LORD our God is the one and only LORD. And you must love the LORD your God with all your heart, all your soul, all your mind, and all your strength.'" Mark 12:29-30

You must not have any other god but me. Exodus 20:3

If you refuse to serve the LORD, then choose today whom you will serve ... But as for me and my family, we will serve the LORD. Joshua 24:15

What are some benefits of living with right priorities?

How joyful are those who fear the LORD – all who follow his ways! You will enjoy the fruit of your labor. How joyful and prosperous you will be! Your wife will be like a fruitful grapevine, flourishing within your home. Your children will be like vigorous young olive trees as they sit around your table. That is the LORD's blessing for those who fear him. Psalm 128:1-4

Those who fear the LORD are secure; he will be a refuge for their children. Proverbs 14:26

Purify me from my sins, and I will be clean; wash me, and I will be whiter than snow. PSALM 51:7

Why is purity so important?

Who may climb the mountain of the LORD? Who may stand in his holy place? Only those whose hands and hearts are pure, who do not worship idols and never tell lies. They will receive the LORD's blessing and have a right relationship with God their savior. Such people may seek you and worship in your presence, O God of Jacob. Psalm 24:3-6

God blesses those whose hearts are pure, for they will see God. Matthew 5:8

If you keep yourself pure, you will be a special utensil for honorable use. Your life will be clean, and you will be ready for the Master to use you for every good work. 2 Timothy 2:21

Teach me your ways, O LORD, that I may live according to your truth! Grant me purity of heart, so that I may honor you. Psalm 86:11

Fix your thoughts on what is true, and honorable, and right, and pure, and lovely, and admirable. Think about things that are excellent and worthy of praise. Philippians 4:8

Regrets

The kind of sorrow God wants us to experience leads us away from sin and results in salvation. There's no regret for that kind of sorrow. 2 CORINTHIANS 7:10

How can I deal with the regrets in my life?

Anyone who belongs to Christ has become a new person. The old life is gone; a new life has begun! 2 Corinthians 5:17

Have mercy on me, O God, because of your unfailing love. Because of your great compassion, blot out the stain of my sins ... Restore to me the joy of your salvation, and make me willing to obey you.
Psalm 51:1, 12

"Come now, let's settle this," says the LORD. "Though your sins are like scarlet, I will make them as white as snow. Though they are red like crimson, I will make them as white as wool." Isaiah 1:18

I have not achieved [perfection], but I focus on this one thing: Forgetting the past and looking forward to what lies ahead, I press on.
Philippians 3:13-14

How can I avoid regrets?

Do to others whatever you would like them to do to you. This is the essence of all that is taught in the law and the prophets. Matthew 7:12

Renewal

[The Lord] renews my strength. He guides me along right paths, bringing honor to his name. PSALM 23:3

My life is a mess, and I feel like I need to make a new start. How can I experience renewal?

Throw off your old sinful nature and your former way of life, which is corrupted by lust and deception. Instead, let the Spirit renew your thoughts and attitudes. Put on your new nature, created to be like God – truly righteous and holy. Ephesians 4:22-24

Create in me a clean heart, O God. Renew a loyal spirit within me. Psalm 51:10

[The sovereign Lord said,] "I will give you a new heart, and I will put a new spirit in you. I will take out your stony, stubborn heart and give you a tender, responsive heart. And I will put my Spirit in you so that you will follow my decrees and be careful to obey my regulations." Ezekiel 36:26-27

Put on your new nature, and be renewed as you learn to know your Creator and become like him. Colossians 3:10

We never give up. Though our bodies are dying, our spirits are being renewed every day. God renews your spirit in spite of your physical troubles. 2 Corinthians 4:16

Repentance

[The Lord said,] "If my people who are called by my name will humble themselves and pray and seek my face and turn from their wicked ways, I will hear from heaven and will forgive their sins and restore their land." 2 CHRONICLES 7:14

Why is repentance necessary?

The Lord your God is gracious and merciful. If you return to him, he will not continue to turn his face from you. 2 Chronicles 30:9

People who conceal their sins will not prosper, but if they confess and turn from them, they will receive mercy. Proverbs 28:13

Let the wicked change their ways and banish the very thought of doing wrong. Let them turn to the Lord that he may have mercy on them. Yes, turn to our God, for he will forgive generously. Isaiah 55:7

Does God's forgiveness always follow true repentance?

Though we are overwhelmed by our sins, you forgive them all. Psalm 65:3

O Lord, you are so good, so ready to forgive, so full of unfailing love for all who ask for your help. Psalm 86:5

Respect

The LORD watches over those who fear him,
those who rely on his unfailing love. PSALM 33:18

How can I show respect to God?

Keep my Sabbath days of rest, and show reverence toward my sanctuary. I am the LORD.   Leviticus 19:30

What does the LORD your God require of you? He requires only that you fear the LORD your God, and live in a way that pleases him, and love him and serve him with all your heart and soul.   Deuteronomy 10:12

[The Lord said,] "You that are near, acknowledge my might!"   Isaiah 33:13

"Don't be afraid," Moses [said], "for God has come in this way to test you, and so that your fear of him will keep you from sinning!"   Exodus 20:20

Do not bring shame on my holy name, for I will display my holiness among the people of Israel. I am the LORD who makes you holy.   Leviticus 22:32

Since we are receiving a Kingdom that is unshakable, let us be thankful and please God by worshiping him with holy fear and awe. For our God is a devouring fire.   Hebrews 12:28-29

Righteousness

We are made right with God by placing our faith in Jesus Christ. And this is true for everyone who believes, no matter who we are. ROMANS 3:22

What is righteousness?

The Scriptures tell us, "Abraham believed God, and God counted him as righteous because of his faith." Romans 4:3

Righteousness is consistently following God's Word and will, being forgiven of sin, walking with God daily, having an unwavering faith in God and his promises, loving him deeply, demonstrating persistent integrity, and avoiding evil.

How can I be considered righteous?

It is by believing in your heart that you are made right with God, and it is by confessing with your mouth that you are saved.
Romans 10:10

Since we have been made right in God's sight by faith, we have peace with God because of what Jesus Christ our Lord has done for us. Because of our faith, Christ has brought us into this place of undeserved privilege where we now stand, and we confidently and joyfully look forward to sharing God's glory. Romans 5:1-2

I no longer count on my own righteousness through obeying the law; rather, I become righteous through faith in Christ. For God's way of making us right with himself depends on faith. Philippians 3:9

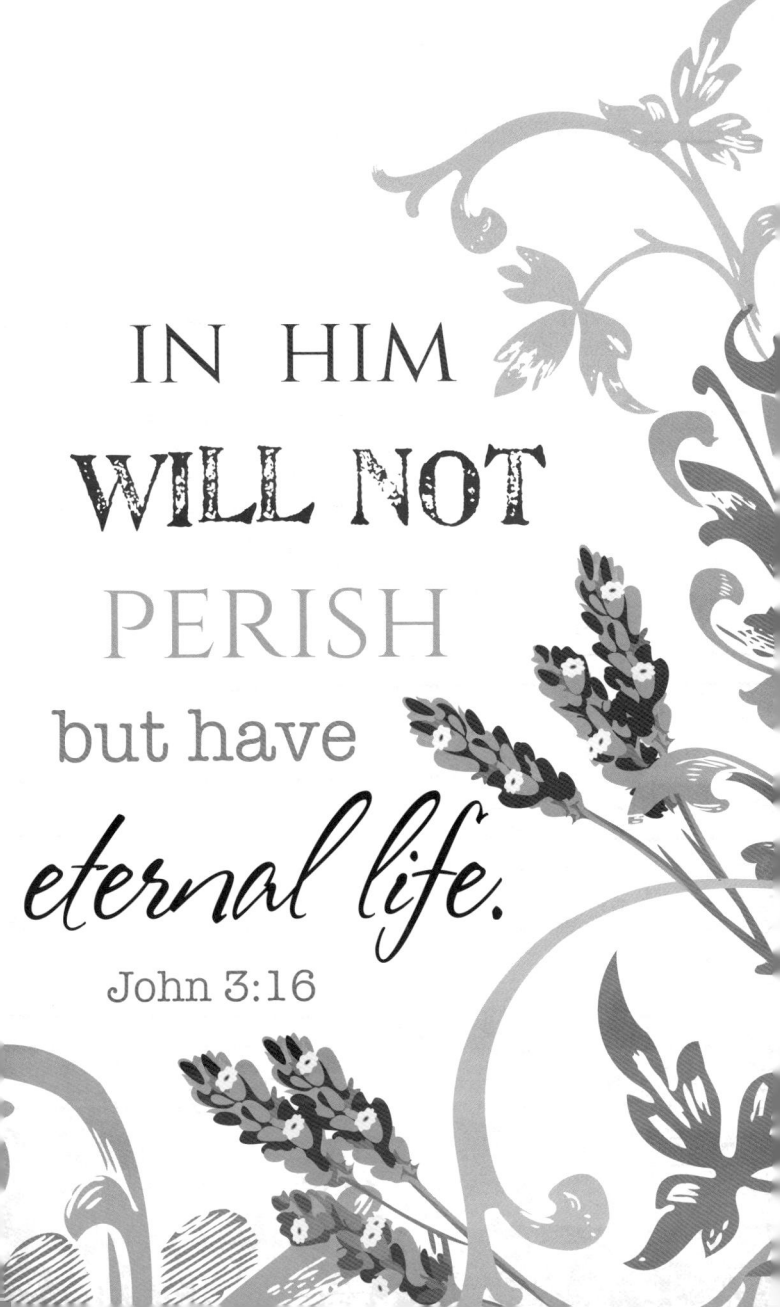

> If you confess with your mouth that Jesus is Lord
> and believe in your heart that God raised him
> from the dead, you will be saved. ROMANS 10:9

How can I be saved?

Everyone who calls on the name of the LORD will be saved.
Romans 10:13

God loved the world so much that he gave his one and only Son, so that everyone who believes in him will not perish but have eternal life.
John 3:16

[Jesus said,] "I tell you the truth, those who listen to my message and believe in God who sent me have eternal life." John 5:24

God's Word promises salvation to those who ask Jesus to forgive their sins. Call out to him and tell him you need him to save you. He promised that if you believe in him, you will be saved.

How can I be sure of my salvation?

To all who believed him and accepted him, he gave the right to become children of God. John 1:12

All who are led by the Spirit of God are children of God. Romans 8:14

Since we have been made right in God's sight by faith, we have peace with God because of what Jesus Christ our Lord has done for us.
Romans 5:1

Security

Those who trust in the LORD are as secure
as Mount Zion; they will not be defeated
but will endure forever. PSALM 125:1

With so much change and instability in the world, how can my faith help me feel secure?

I waited patiently for the LORD to help me, and he turned to me and heard my cry. He lifted me out of the pit of despair, out of the mud and the mire. He set my feet on solid ground and steadied me as I walked along. Psalm 40:1-2

[Jesus said,] "Anyone who listens to my teaching and follows it is wise, like a person who builds a house on solid rock. Though the rain comes in torrents and the floodwaters rise and the winds beat against that house, it won't collapse because it is built on bedrock." Matthew 7:24-25

How does God provide security?

We have a priceless inheritance – an inheritance that is kept in heaven for you, pure and undefiled, beyond the reach of change and decay. And through your faith, God is protecting you by his power until you receive this salvation, which is ready to be revealed on the last day for all to see. 1 Peter 1:4-5

God is our refuge and strength, always ready to help in times of trouble. So we will not fear when earthquakes come and the mountains crumble into the sea. Psalm 46:1-2

Service

> Those who care nothing for their life in this world will keep it for eternity ... And the Father will honor anyone who serves me. JOHN 12:25-26

How can I serve God today?

Choose today whom you will serve ... As for me and my family, we will serve the LORD. Joshua 24:15

Love the LORD your God, walk in all his ways, obey his commands, hold firmly to him, and serve him with all your heart and all your soul. Joshua 22:5

There are different kinds of spiritual gifts, but the same Spirit is the source of them all. There are different kinds of service, but we serve the same Lord ... A spiritual gift is given to each of us so we can help each other. 1 Corinthians 12:4-5, 7

How did Jesus serve?

Whoever wants to be a leader among you must be your servant ... For even the Son of Man came not to be served but to serve others and to give his life as a ransom for many. Matthew 20:26, 28

You must have the same attitude that Christ Jesus had. Though he was God, he did not think of equality with God as something to cling to. Instead, he gave up his divine privileges; he took the humble position of a slave and was born as a human being. Philippians 2:5-7

Significance

What are mere mortals that you should think about them, human beings that you should care for them? Yet you made them only a little lower than God and crowned them with glory and honor. PSALM 8:4-5

What are some of the most significant things in life?

If I had the gift of prophecy, and if I understood all of God's secret plans and possessed all knowledge, and if I had such faith that I could move mountains, but didn't love others, I would be nothing. If I gave everything I have to the poor and even sacrificed my body, I could boast about it; but if I didn't love others, I would have gained nothing. 1 Corinthians 13:2-3

My life is worth nothing to me unless I use it for finishing the work assigned me by the Lord Jesus – the work of telling others the Good News about the wonderful grace of God. Acts 20:24

Everything else is worthless when compared with the infinite value of knowing Christ Jesus my Lord. For his sake I have discarded everything else, counting it all as garbage, so that I could gain Christ. Philippians 3:8

How can I cope with feelings of insignificance?

What is the price of two sparrows – one copper coin? But not a single sparrow can fall to the ground without your Father knowing it. And the very hairs on your head are all numbered. So don't be afraid; you are more valuable to God than a whole flock of sparrows. Matthew 10:29-31

> The words of the godly are a
> life-giving fountain. PROVERBS 10:11

What kinds of words should I speak?

Let everything you say be good and helpful, so that your words will be an encouragement to those who hear them. Ephesians 4:29

Gentle words are a tree of life. Proverbs 15:4

Don't repay evil for evil. Don't retaliate with insults when people insult you. Instead, pay them back with a blessing. That is what God has called you to do, and he will bless you for it. 1 Peter 3:9

What kinds of words should I avoid speaking?

Does anyone want to live a life that is long and prosperous? Then keep your tongue from speaking evil and your lips from telling lies!
Psalm 34:12-13

Don't speak evil against each other, dear brothers and sisters. If you criticize and judge each other, then you are criticizing and judging God's law. James 4:11

Fools vent their anger, but the wise quietly hold it back. Proverbs 29:11

Spiritual Warfare

> Put on all of God's armor so that you will be able to stand firm against all strategies of the devil. EPHESIANS 6:11

What does the Bible say about spiritual warfare?

Stay alert! Watch out for your great enemy, the devil. He prowls around like a roaring lion, looking for someone to devour. 1 Peter 5:8

For we are not fighting against flesh-and-blood enemies, but against evil rulers and authorities of the unseen world, against mighty powers in this dark world, and against evil spirits in the heavenly places. Ephesians 6:12

At the name of Jesus every knee should bow, in heaven and on earth and under the earth. Philippians 2:10

Resist the devil, and he will flee from you. James 4:7

Jesus was led by the Spirit into the wilderness to be tempted there by the devil … During that time the devil came and said to him, "If you are the Son of God, tell these stones to become loaves of bread." But Jesus told him, "No! The Scriptures say …" Matthew 4:1, 3-4

When you resist the devil in the name and power of Jesus, the devil will flee from you. At the name of Jesus, Satan has no power.

Don't be afraid, for I am with you. Don't be discouraged, for I am your God. I will strengthen you and help you. I will hold you up with my victorious right hand. ISAIAH 41:10

What causes stress?

When troubles come your way, consider it an opportunity for great joy. For you know that when your faith is tested, your endurance has a chance to grow. So let it grow, for when your endurance is fully developed, you will be perfect and complete, needing nothing.
James 1:2-4

Adversity and the normal problems of life cause stress.

How can I deal with stress?

Give your burdens to the LORD, and he will take care of you. He will not permit the godly to slip and fall.   Psalm 55:22

[Jesus said,] "Don't let your hearts be troubled. Trust in God, and trust also in me."   John 14:1

The first step in dealing with stress is to bring your burdens to the Lord. Only he can bring true peace of heart and mind. God's availability and promises are effective stress reducers.

Submission

> When people do not accept divine guidance, they run wild. But whoever obeys the law is joyful. PROVERBS 29:18

What is submission to God?

Jesus ... prayed, "My Father! If this cup cannot be taken away unless I drink it, your will be done." Matthew 26:42

Submission involves seeking God's will and following it wholeheartedly out of a genuine love and deep respect for him.

To whom should I submit?

Do not let any part of your body become an instrument of evil to serve sin. Instead, give yourselves completely to God, for you were dead, but now you have new life. So use your whole body as an instrument to do what is right for the glory of God.
Romans 6:13

Since we respected our earthly fathers who disciplined us, shouldn't we submit even more to the discipline of the Father of our spirits, and live forever? Hebrews 12:9

Submit to one another out of reverence for Christ. For wives, this means submit to your husbands as to the Lord. Ephesians 5:21-22

Everyone must submit to governing authorities. For all authority comes from God, and those in positions of authority have been placed there by God. Romans 13:1

Suffering

All praise to God, the Father of our Lord Jesus Christ. God is our merciful Father and the source of all comfort. He comforts us in all our troubles so that we can comfort others. When they are troubled, we will be able to give them the same comfort God has given us. 2 CORINTHIANS 1:3-4

Why am I suffering? Doesn't God care about me?

When your faith is tested, your endurance has a chance to grow. James 1:3

We can rejoice, too, when we run into problems and trials, for we know that they help us develop endurance. And endurance develops strength of character. Romans 5:3-4

How do I stay close to God in times of suffering?

Since we are his children, we are his heirs. In fact, together with Christ we are heirs of God's glory. But if we are to share his glory, we must also share his suffering. Yet what we suffer now is nothing compared to the glory he will reveal to us later. Romans 8:17-18

Since [Jesus] himself has gone through suffering and testing, he is able to help us when we are being tested. Hebrews 2:18

Temptation

The temptations in your life are no different from what others experience. And God is faithful. He will not allow the temptation to be more than you can stand. When you are tempted, he will show you a way out so that you can endure. 1 CORINTHIANS 10:13

Is temptation sin?

[Jesus] faced all of the same testings we do, yet he did not sin. Hebrews 4:15

Jesus was severely tempted, yet he never gave in to temptation. Since Jesus was tempted and remained sinless, we know that being tempted is not the same as sinning.

Does temptation ever come from God?

When you are being tempted, do not say, "God is tempting me." God is never tempted to do wrong, and he never tempts anyone else. James 1:13

Resist the devil, and he will flee from you. James 4:7

Stay alert! Watch out for your great enemy, the devil. He prowls around like a roaring lion, looking for someone to devour. Stand firm against him, and be strong in your faith. 1 Peter 5:8-9

Temptation originates not in the mind of God but in the mind of Satan, who plants it in your heart. Victory over temptation originates in the mind of God and flows to your heart.

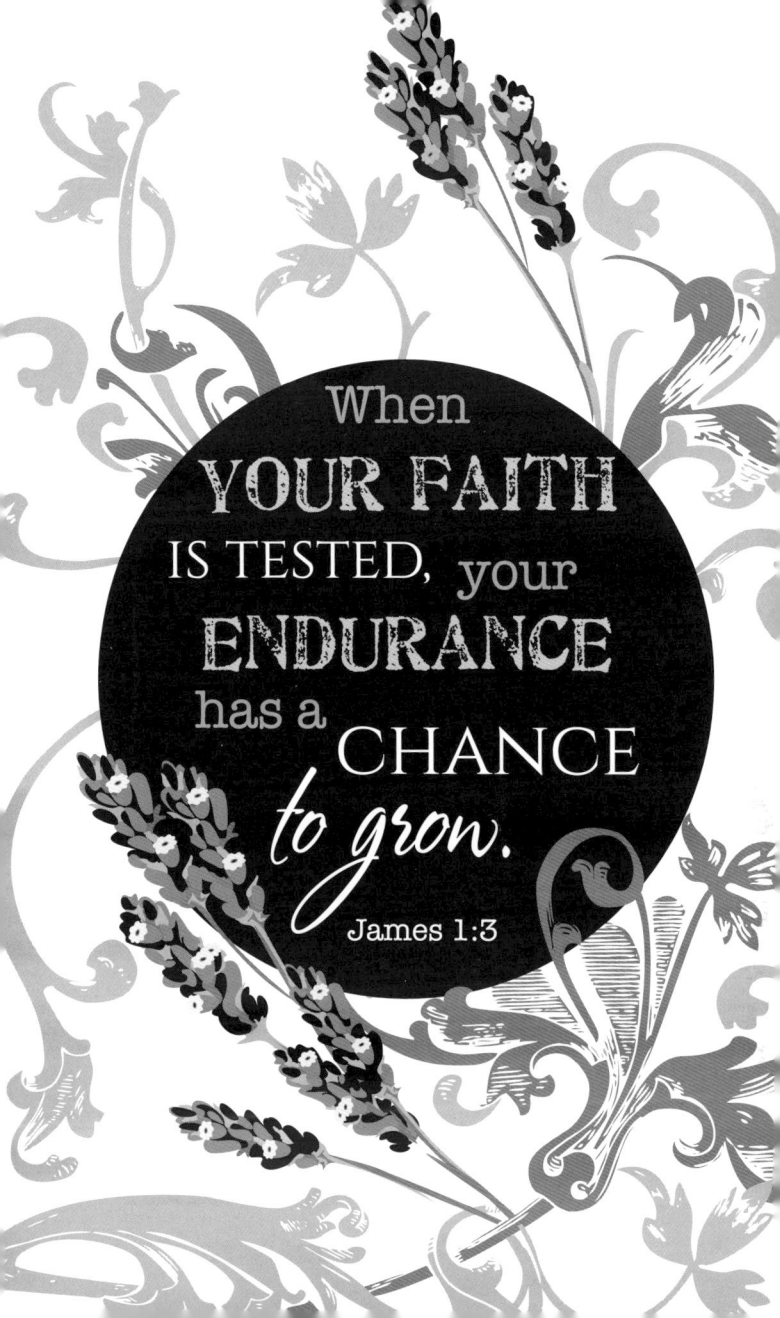

> God blesses those who patiently endure testing and temptation. Afterward they will receive the crown of life that God has promised to those who love him. JAMES 1:12

How is testing different from temptation?

These trials will show that your faith is genuine. It is being tested as fire tests and purifies gold – though your faith is far more precious than mere gold. 1 Peter 1:7

When your faith is tested, your endurance has a chance to grow. James 1:3

Satan tempts to destroy your faith; God tests to strengthen and purify it. Temptations try to make you quit. Testing tries to help you endure and not quit.

What good comes out of being tested?

When troubles come your way, consider it an opportunity for great joy. For you know that when your faith is tested, your endurance has a chance to grow. So let it grow, for when your endurance is fully developed, you will be perfect and complete, needing nothing. James 1:2-4

The LORD your God is testing you to see if you truly love him with all your heart and soul. Deuteronomy 13:3

Thankfulness

> Give thanks to the Lord, for he is good! His faithful love endures forever. 1 CHRONICLES 16:34

How can I express my thankfulness?

Sing psalms and hymns and spiritual songs to God with thankful hearts. Colossians 3:16

Praise the Lord! I will thank the Lord with all my heart as I meet with his godly people. How amazing are the deeds of the Lord! All who delight in him should ponder them. Psalm 111:1-2

Devote yourselves to prayer with an alert mind and a thankful heart. Colossians 4:2

Let all that I am praise the Lord. O Lord my God, how great you are! You are robed with honor and majesty. Psalm 104:1

For what can I always be thankful, regardless of circumstances?

I thank Christ Jesus our Lord, who has given me strength to do his work. He considered me trustworthy and appointed me to serve him. 1 Timothy 1:12

God saved you by his grace when you believed … It is a gift from God. Ephesians 2:8

Timing of God

This vision is for a future time. It describes the end, and it will be fulfilled. If it seems slow in coming, wait patiently, for it will surely take place. It will not be delayed. HABAKKUK 2:3

Can I trust God's timing in my life?

You made all the delicate, inner parts of my body and knit me together in my mother's womb. Psalm 139:13

O LORD, I will honor and praise your name, for you are my God. You do such wonderful things! You planned them long ago, and now you have accomplished them. Isaiah 25:1

God had your whole life planned before you were even born. He knows everything about you and is qualified and can be trusted to intervene on your behalf. His agenda and his timing for you are perfect.

How can I best wait for God's timing?

As soon as I pray, you answer me; you encourage me by giving me strength. Psalm 138:3

Rejoice in our confident hope. Be patient in trouble, and keep on praying. Romans 12:12

I keep praying to you, LORD ... In your unfailing love, O God, answer my prayer with your sure salvation. Psalm 69:13

Trust

You will keep in perfect peace all who trust in you, all whose thoughts are fixed on you! ISAIAH 26:3

What does it mean to trust God?

In him our hearts rejoice, for we trust in his holy name.   Psalm 33:21

You are worthy, O Lord our God, to receive glory and honor and power. For you created all things.   Revelation 4:11

Trusting God means recognizing that he is worthy of your trust and praise.

How joyful are those who fear the LORD and delight in obeying his commands.   Psalm 112:1

Though you do not see him now, you trust him; and you rejoice with a glorious, inexpressible joy.   1 Peter 1:8

Trusting God and obeying him will bring you joy.

Anyone who believes in God's Son has eternal life.   John 3:36

No one will ever be made right with God by obeying the law. Galatians 2:16

Trusting God means depending on Jesus Christ alone for salvation. And trusting Christ for salvation means ceasing to trust in your own efforts to be righteous.

> The very essence of your words is truth; all your just regulations will stand forever. PSALM 119:160

How does truth impact my relationship with God?

[The] truth gives [those whom God has chosen] confidence that they have eternal life, which God – who does not lie – promised them before the world began. Titus 1:2

Those who are honest and fair, who refuse to profit by fraud, who stay far away from bribes … who shut their eyes to all enticement to do wrong – these are the ones who will dwell on high. Isaiah 33:15-16

Jesus [said], "I am the way, the truth, and the life. No one can come to the Father except through me." John 14:6

God wants you to accept the truth that only by following Jesus can you spend eternity with him. He wants to spare you from the terrible consequences of pushing this most important truth away.

Why is telling the truth so important?

Truthful words stand the test of time, but lies are soon exposed. Proverbs 12:19

If you are faithful in little things, you will be faithful in large ones. But if you are dishonest in little things, you won't be honest with greater responsibilities. Luke 16:10

All of you can join together with one voice, giving praise and glory to God, the Father of our Lord Jesus Christ. ROMANS 15:6

What is true unity?

[Jesus said,] "I am the good shepherd ... I have other sheep, too, that are not in this sheepfold. I must bring them also. They will listen to my voice, and there will be one flock with one shepherd." John 10:14, 16

Just as our bodies have many parts and each part has a special function, so it is with Christ's body. We are many parts of one body, and we all belong to each other. Romans 12:4-5

There is no longer Jew or Gentile, slave or free, male and female. For you are all one in Christ Jesus. Galatians 3:28

Why is unity important?

I appeal to you, dear brothers and sisters, by the authority of our Lord Jesus Christ, to live in harmony with each other. Let there be no divisions in the church. Rather, be of one mind, united in thought and purpose. 1 Corinthians 1:10

How wonderful and pleasant it is when brothers live together in harmony! Psalm 133:1

Unity creates a more beautiful worship experience.

Vulnerability

When we were utterly helpless, Christ came at just the right time and died for us sinners. ROMANS 5:6

How do I keep myself from being vulnerable to harm?

Look, I will come as unexpectedly as a thief! Blessed are all who are watching for me, who keep their clothing ready so they will not have to walk around naked and ashamed. Revelation 16:15

If you are fully prepared for Christ's coming, you will not be vulnerable to God's wrath on Judgment Day.

Is God vulnerable in any way?

I will give him the honors of a victorious soldier, because he exposed himself to death. He was counted among the rebels. He bore the sins of many and interceded for rebels. Isaiah 53:12

Jesus was led by the Spirit into the wilderness to be tempted there by the devil. Matthew 4:1

God, in Christ, made himself vulnerable to abuse and death at the hands of evil people. Jesus also made himself vulnerable to temptation, but he resisted.

Weariness

He gives power to the weak and strength to the powerless. Even youths will become weak and tired, and young men will fall in exhaustion. But those who trust in the LORD will find new strength. They will soar high on wings like eagles. They will run and not grow weary. They will walk and not faint. ISAIAH 40:29-31

Who can help me when I am tired?

The Sovereign LORD is my strength! He makes me as surefooted as a deer, able to tread upon the heights. Habakkuk 3:19

Jesus said, "Come to me, all of you who are weary and carry heavy burdens, and I will give you rest." Matthew 11:28

[God] said, "My grace is all you need. My power works best in weakness." So now I am glad to boast about my weaknesses, so that the power of Christ can work through me. 2 Corinthians 12:9

[The Lord said,] "I have given rest to the weary and joy to the sorrowing." Jeremiah 31:25

Think of all the hostility [Jesus] endured from sinful people; then you won't become weary and give up ... So take a new grip with your tired hands and strengthen your weak knees. Hebrews 12:3, 12

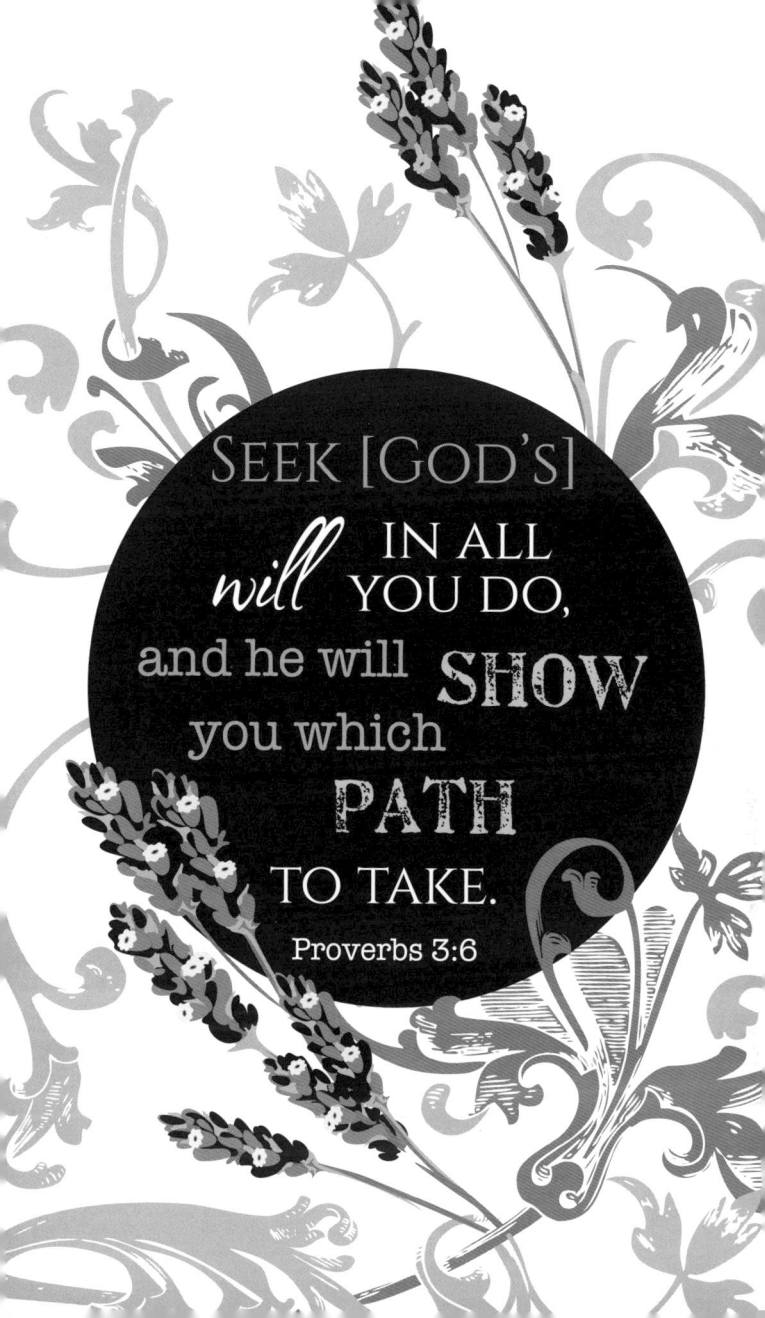

Will of God

> Seek [God's] will in all you do, and he will show you which path to take. PROVERBS 3:6

Does God really have a plan for my life?

I am certain that God, who began the good work within you, will continue his work until it is finally finished on the day when Christ Jesus returns. Philippians 1:6

"I know the plans I have for you," says the LORD. "They are plans for good and not for disaster, to give you a future and a hope." Jeremiah 29:11

The LORD will work out his plans for my life. Psalm 138:8

What can I do to discover God's will for my life?

Come, let us go up to the mountain of the LORD, to the house of Jacob's God. There he will teach us his ways, and we will walk in his paths. Isaiah 2:3

If you need wisdom, ask our generous God, and he will give it to you. He will not rebuke you for asking. James 1:5

We are confident that he hears us whenever we ask for anything that pleases him. 1 John 5:14

Actively seek God's will through prayer, reading the Bible, conversation with mature believers and reliable advisers, and discernment of the circumstances around you.

Wisdom

I will certainly give you the wisdom and knowledge you requested. 2 CHRONICLES 1:12

How can I obtain wisdom?

Fear of the LORD is the foundation of wisdom. Knowledge of the Holy One results in good judgment.   Proverbs 9:10

You have received the Holy Spirit, and he lives within you, so you don't need anyone to teach you what is true. For the Spirit teaches you everything you need to know, and what he teaches is true – it is not a lie. So just as he has taught you, remain in fellowship with Christ.   1 John 2:27

Let the wise listen to these proverbs and become even wiser. Let those with understanding receive guidance by exploring the meaning in these proverbs and parables, the words of the wise and their riddles.   Proverbs 1:5-6

If you need wisdom, ask our generous God, and he will give it to you. He will not rebuke you for asking.   James 1:5

Teach me your ways, O LORD, that I may live according to your truth! Grant me purity of heart, so that I may honor you.
Psalm 86:11

Following Christ's teachings and obeying his words will give wisdom.

How beautiful are the feet of messengers
who bring good news! ROMANS 10:15

How can I overcome my fear of witnessing?

[Jesus said,] "I will give you the right words and such wisdom that none of your opponents will be able to reply or refute you!" Luke 21:15

The LORD is my light and my salvation – so why should I be afraid? The LORD is my fortress, protecting me from danger, so why should I tremble? Psalm 27:1

Anyone who wants to be my disciple must follow me, because my servants must be where I am. And the Father will honor anyone who serves me. John 12:26

You will receive power when the Holy Spirit comes upon you. And you will be my witnesses, telling people about me everywhere … to the ends of the earth. Acts 1:8

What do I do when people aren't interested in hearing about Jesus?

Preach the word of God. Be prepared, whether the time is favorable or not. 2 Timothy 4:2

If circumstances or people's attitudes are not favorable, speak out anyway and tell people what Jesus has done in your life.

Worry

Give all your worries and cares to God,
for he cares about you. 1 PETER 5:7

How can I worry less?

Don't worry about anything; instead, pray about everything.
Philippians 4:6

[God] alone is my rock and my salvation, my fortress where I will not be shaken. Psalm 62:6

Can all your worries add a single moment to your life? Matthew 6:27

Instead of adding more time or a better quality of life, worry affects your health and kills your joy.

When does worry become sin?

The seed that fell among the thorns represents those who hear God's word, but all too quickly the message is crowded out by the worries of this life and the lure of wealth, so no fruit is produced. Matthew 13:22

Think about the things of heaven, not the things of earth. Colossians 3:2

Worry over the concerns of life becomes sin when it prevents the Word of God from taking root in your life.

Worship

God elevated him to the place of highest honor and gave him the name above all other names, that at the name of Jesus every knee should bow, in heaven and on earth and under the earth, and every tongue confess that Jesus Christ is Lord, to the glory of God the Father. PHILIPPIANS 2:9-11

How is worship integral to my relationship with God?

Give to the LORD the glory he deserves! Bring your offering and come into his presence. Worship the LORD in all his holy splendor. 1 Chronicles 16:29

Great is the LORD! He is most worthy of praise! No one can measure his greatness. Psalm 145:3

Come, let us worship and bow down. Let us kneel before the LORD our maker. Psalm 95:6

Since we are receiving a Kingdom that is unshakable, let us be thankful and please God by worshiping him with holy fear and awe. Hebrews 12:28

Worship is the recognition of who God is and who you are in relation to him. It is acknowledging his character and his many acts of love toward you. And it is returning love to him.

Worth

> [The Lord] made [human beings] only
> a little lower than God and crowned them
> with glory and honor. PSALM 8:5

What am I worth – what is my value to God?

God created human beings in his own image. In the image of God he created them; male and female he created them.
Genesis 1:27

We are God's masterpiece. He has created us anew in Christ Jesus, so we can do the good things he planned for us long ago.
Ephesians 2:10

You made all the delicate, inner parts of my body and knit me together in my mother's womb.   Psalm 139:13

You are all children of God through faith in Christ Jesus.
Galatians 3:26

God made you in his own image – you are his treasure and masterpiece! You are invaluable to him.

What makes me worthy?

God bought you with a high price. So you must honor God with your body. 1 Corinthians 6:20

You are worthy because God paid a high price for you. He loved you enough to die for you.

Index

Abilities	4
Acceptance	5
Adoption	6
Affirmation	7
Anger	8
Appearance	9
Bible	10
Blessings	12
Boundaries	13
Busyness	14
Celebration	15
Change	18
Christlikeness	19
Church	20
Comfort	22
Complaining	23
Compromise	24
Conflict	25
Confrontation	26
Contentment	27
Crisis	30
Criticism	31
Disappointment	32
Discipline	33
Divorce	34
Emotions	35
Encouragement	36
Escape	38
Expectations	39
Failure	40
Faith	42
Family	43
Forgiveness	44
Friendship	46
Frustration	47
Gentleness	48
Gossip	49
Grief	50
Healing	51
Health	52
Home	53
Hope	54
Hospitality	56
Humility	57
Husbands	58
Infertility	59
Intimacy	60
Joy	62
Kindness	63
Listening	64
Loneliness	65
Loss	66
Love	68
Marriage	69
Meditation	70
Mercy	71
Mistakes	72
Modesty	73
Money	74
Mothers	75
Motives	76
Needs	77

Neighbors	80
Obedience	81
Parenting	82
Patience	84
Poverty	85
Praise	86
Prayer	87
Priorities	88
Purity	89
Regrets	90
Renewal	92
Repentance	93
Respect	94
Righteousness	95
Salvation	98
Security	99
Service	100
Significance	101
Speech	102
Spiritual Warfare	103
Stress	104
Submission	106
Suffering	107
Temptation	108
Testing	110
Thankfulness	111
Timing of God	112
Trust	113
Truth	114
Unity	116
Vulnerability	117
Weariness	118
Will of God	120
Wisdom	121
Witnessing	122
Worry	123
Worship	124
Worth	125